V. S. NAIPAUL

FINDING THE CENTRE

Two Narratives

 ANDRE DEUTSCH

First published 1984 by
André Deutsch Limited
105 Great Russell Street London WC1

British Library Cataloguing in Publication Data

Naipaul, V. S.
    Finding the centre
    1. Naipaul, V. S.   2. Authors, Trinidadian—
    20th century—Biography
    I. title
    813   PR9272.9.N32Z/

    ISBN 0 233 97664 7

Typeset by Gloucester Typesetting Services
Printed in Great Britain by
Ebenezer Baylis & Son Ltd
The Trinity Press, Worcester, and London

FINDING THE CENTRE

Two Narratives

Contents

AUTHOR'S FOREWORD

The two personal narrative pieces that make up *Finding the Centre* were written one after the other and occupied the best part of two years. They are offered as a book principally for that reason; and also because, over and above their story content, both pieces are about the process of writing. Both pieces seek in different ways to admit the reader to that process.

'Prologue to an Autobiography' is what its title says. It is not an autobiography, a story of a life or deeds done. It is an account of something less easily seized: my literary beginnings and the imaginative promptings of my many-sided background. The idea of such a work first came to me early one morning in 1967 in a second-class Bombay hotel. If I were a poet the impulse might have produced a poem. To a prose writer, though, the impulse by itself was nothing. It needed a story, and I could think of none for some years. This was just as well: my knowledge of my background, as I was to find out, was incomplete. In Trinidad in 1972 (as the present story obliquely records) I did a lot of reading and looking around. I thought I had found a story; I began to write. After three months my narrative ran into the sands. It had no centre. I hadn't yet found the story that would do the narrative binding – gather together all the strands of my background – and achieve the particular truth I had in mind. The project, by that time the work of perhaps half a year, was set aside.

More than four years later, in 1977, I went to Venezuela.

While I was there I visited the man who had inspired my very first story. I was moved, but the note I wanted to make about the visit refused to be written. I didn't get to the end of the first sentence. Water fell on my open notebook soon afterwards; the ink ran, the paper crinkled; the notebook was put away and never used again. So the experience stayed with me, untouched by words, its references unexplored.

Four and a half years later, in 1981, under the goading of an American editor, Richard Locke, who wanted me to do something substantial for him, the Venezuelan experience came back to me, and I saw it as the centre of the narrative I had set aside more than eight years before. I saw – and, after all the thought, it seemed so obvious – that an account of my literary beginnings could begin, quite directly, with the writing of my first story: to that point my narrative could circle back, taking in all the things I wanted to lay out. I worked out the story in my head for the next three or four months; revisited some of the places I was going to write about; and then, feeling fairly secure, I began to write. The present piece is what resulted. It represents my full intention. As a story of discovery and growing knowledge, it goes beyond the impulse felt all those years ago in Bombay.

If 'Prologue to an Autobiography' is an account, with the understanding of middle age, of the writer's beginnings, 'The Crocodiles of Yamoussoukro' shows this writer, in his latest development, going about one side of his business: travelling, adding to his knowledge of the world, exposing himself to new people and new relationships. 'The Crocodiles of Yamoussoukro' is about the Ivory Coast. But the people I found, the people I was attracted to, were not unlike myself. They too were trying to find order in their world, looking for the centre; and my discovery of these people is as much part of the story as the unfolding of the West African background. A writer after a time carries his world with him, his own burden of experience, human experience and literary experience (one deepening the other); and I do believe – especially after writing 'Prologue to an Autobiography' – that I would have found equivalent connections with my past and myself wherever I had gone.

When more than twenty years ago I began to travel as a writer, I was uneasy and uncertain. My instinct was towards fiction; I found it constricting to have to deal with fact. I was glamoured by the idea of the long journey, but I had no idea how I might set about looking at a place in a way that would be of value to other people. My brief – which was to look at various colonial territories in the Caribbean and South America – was political-cultural in intention. But I had no views or opinions, no system. I was interested in history; but I was also interested in landscape; above all, I was interested – at times frivolously – in people as I found them.

When it came to the writing, I was uncertain about the value I should give to the traveller's 'I'. This kind of direct participation came awkwardly to me, and the literary problem was also partly a personal one. In 1960 I was still a colonial, travelling to far-off places that were still colonies, in a world still more or less ruled by colonial ideas. In Surinam in 1961, in a banana plantation (curiously quiet, the mulch of rotting banana trash thick and soft and muffling underfoot), the Indian official who – with a Dutch technical expert in attendance – was showing me around broke off to say in a semi-conspiratorial way, 'You are the first one of us to come out on a mission like this.'

To travel was glamorous. But travel also made unsuspected demands on me as a man and a writer, and perhaps for that reason it soon became a necessary stimulus for me. It broadened my world view; it showed me a changing world and took me out of my own colonial shell; it became the substitute for the mature social experience – the deepening knowledge of a society – which my background and the nature of my life denied me. My uncertainty about my role withered; a role was not necessary. I recognized my own instincts as a traveller, and was content to be myself, to be what I had always been, a looker. And I learned to look in my own way.

To arrive at a place without knowing anyone there, and sometimes without an introduction; to learn how to move among strangers for the short time one could afford to be among them; to hold oneself in constant readiness for adventure or revelation; to allow oneself to be carried along, up to a point, by accidents; and consciously to follow up other impulses – that could be as creative and imaginative a procedure as the writing that came after. Travel of this sort became an intense experience for me. It used all the sides of my personality; I was always wound up. There were no rules. Every place visited was different; every place opened in a new way. Always, at the beginning, there was the possibility of failure – of not finding anything, not getting started on the chain of accidents and encounters. This gave a gambler's excitement to every arrival. My luck held; perhaps I made it hold. Always, after the tension, there came a moment when a place began to clear up, and certain incidents (some of them disregarded until then) began to have meaning.

I would have liked in 'The Crocodiles of Yamoussoukro'

to take the reader through all the stages of my adventure in the Ivory Coast. I would have liked to begin at the very beginning, with the blankness and anxiety of arrival. But it didn't work as narrative. And narrative was my aim. Within that, my travelling method was intended to be transparent. The reader will see how the material was gathered; he will also see how the material could have served fiction or political journalism or a travelogue. But the material here serves itself alone: 'The Crocodiles of Yamoussoukro' offers the experience of travel and human discovery for its own sake. All that was added later was understanding. Out of that understanding the narrative came. However creatively one travels, however deep an experience in childhood or middle age, it takes thought (a sifting of impulses, ideas and references that become more multifarious as one grows older) to understand what one has lived through or where one has been.

PROLOGUE TO AN AUTOBIOGRAPHY

I

It is now nearly thirty years since, in a BBC room in London, on an old BBC typewriter, and on smooth, 'non-rustle' BBC script paper, I wrote the first sentence of my first publishable book. I was some three months short of my twenty-third birthday. I had left Oxford ten months before, and was living in London, trying to keep afloat and, in between, hoping to alleviate my anxiety but always only adding to it, trying to get started as a writer.

At Oxford I had been supported by a Trinidad government scholarship. In London I was on my own. The only money I got – eight guineas a week, less 'deductions' – came from the BBC Caribbean Service. My only piece of luck in the past year, and even in the past two years, had been to get a part-time job editing and presenting a weekly literary programme for the Caribbean.

The Caribbean Service was on the second floor of what had been the Langham Hotel, opposite Broadcasting House. On this floor the BBC had set aside a room for people like me, 'freelances' – to me then not a word suggesting freedom and valour, but suggesting only people on the fringe of a mighty enterprise, a depressed and suppliant class: I would have given a lot to be 'staff'.

The freelances' room didn't encourage thoughts of radio glory; it was strictly for the production of little scripts. Something of the hotel atmosphere remained: in the great Victorian-Edwardian days of the Langham Hotel (it was mentioned in at least one Sherlock Holmes story), the free-lances' room might have been a pantry. It was at the back of the heavy brick building, and gloomy when the ceiling lights were turned off. It wasn't cheerful when the lights were on: ochre walls with a pea-green dado, the gloss paint tarnished; a radiator below the window, with grit on the sill; two or three chairs, a telephone, two tables and two old standard typewriters.

It was in that Victorian-Edwardian gloom, and at one of those typewriters, that late one afternoon, without having any idea where I was going, and not perhaps intending to type to the end of the page, I wrote: *Every morning when he got up Hat would sit on the banister of his back verandah and shout across, 'What happening there, Bogart?'*

That was a Port of Spain memory. It seemed to come from far back, but it was only eleven or twelve years old. It came from the time when we – various branches of my mother's family – were living in Port of Spain, in a house that belonged to my mother's mother. We were country people, Indians, culturally still Hindus; and this move to Port of Spain was in the nature of a migration: from the Hindu and Indian countryside to the white-negro-mulatto town.

Hat was our neighbour on the street. He wasn't negro or mulatto. But we thought of him as half-way there. He was a Port of Spain Indian. The Port of Spain Indians – there were pockets of them – had no country roots, were individuals, hardly a community, and were separate from us for an additional reason: many of them were Madrassis, descendants of South Indians, not Hindi-speaking, and not people of caste. We didn't see in them any of our own formalities or restrictions; and though we lived raggedly ourselves (and were far too numerous for the house), we thought of the other Indians in the street only as street people.

That shout of 'Bogart!' was in more than one way a shout from the street. And, to add to the incongruity, it was addressed to someone in our yard: a young man, very quiet, yet another person connected in some way with my mother's family. He had come not long before from the country and was living in the separate one-room building at the back of our yard.

We called this room the 'servant room'. Port of Spain houses, up to the 1930s, were built with these separate servant rooms – verandah-less little boxes, probably descended in style from the ancillary 'negro-houses' of slave times. I suppose that in one or two houses in our street servants of the house actually lived in the servant room. But generally it wasn't so. Servant rooms, because of the privacy they offered, were in demand, and not by servants.

It was wartime. The migration of my own family into the town had become part of a more general movement. People of all conditions were coming into Port of Spain to work at the two American bases. One of those bases had been built on recently reclaimed land just at the end of our street – eight houses down. Twice a day we heard the bugles; Americans, formal in their uniforms, with their khaki ties tucked into their shirts, were another part of the life of our street. The street was busy; the yards were crowded. Our yard was more crowded than most. No servant ever lodged in our servant room. Instead, the room sheltered a succession of favoured transients, on their way to better things. Before the big family rush, some of these transients had been outsiders; but now they were mostly relations or people close to the family, like Bogart.

The connection of Bogart with my mother's family was unusual. At the turn of the century Bogart's father and my mother's father had travelled out together from India as indentured immigrants. At some time during the long and frightening journey they had sworn a bond of brotherhood; that was the bond that was being honoured by their descendants.

Bogart's people were from the Punjab, and handsome. The two brothers we had got to know were ambitious men, rising in white-collar jobs. One was a teacher; the other (who had passed through the servant room) was a weekend sportsman who, in the cricket season, regularly got his name in the paper. Bogart didn't have the education or the ambition of his brothers; it wasn't clear what he did for a living. He was placid, without any pronounced character, detached, and in that crowded yard oddly solitary.

Once he went away. When he came back, some weeks or months later, it was said that he had been 'working on a ship'. Port of Spain was a colonial port, and we thought of sailors as very rough, the dregs. So this business of working on a ship – though it suggested money as well as luck, for the jobs were not easy to come by – also held suggestions of danger. It was something for the reckless and the bohemian. But it must have suited Bogart, because after a time he went away – disappeared – again.

There was a story this time that he had gone to Venezuela. He came back; but I had no memory of his return. His adventures – if he had had any – remained unknown to me. I believe I was told that the first time he had gone away, to work on the ship, he had worked as a cook. But that might have been a story I made up myself. All that I knew of Bogart while he lived in the servant room was what, as a child, I saw from a distance. He and his comings and goings were part of the confusion and haphazardness and crowd of that time.

I saw a little more of him four or five years later. The war was over. The American base at the end of the street was closed. The buildings were pulled down, and the local contractor, who knew someone in our family, gave us the run of the place for a few days, to pick up what timber we wanted. My mother's extended family was breaking up into its component parts; we were all leaving my grandmother's house. My father had bought a house of his own; I used timber from the old American base to make a new front gate. Soon I had got the Trinidad government scholarship that was to take me to Oxford.

Bogart was still reportedly a traveller. And in Trinidad now he was able to do what perhaps he had always wanted to do: to put as much distance as possible between himself and people close to him. He was living in Carenage, a seaside village five miles or so west of Port of Spain. Carenage was a negro-mulatto place, with a Spanish flavour (*'pagnol*, in the local French patois). There were few Indians in Carenage; that would have suited Bogart.

With nothing to do, waiting to go away, I was restless, and I sometimes cycled out to Carenage. It was pleasant after the hot ride to splash about in the rocky sea, and pleasant after that to go and have a Coca-Cola at Bogart's. He lived in a side street, a wandering lane, with yards that were half bush, half built-up. He was a tailor now, apparently with customers; and he sat at his machine in his open shop, welcoming but undemonstrative, as placid, as without conversation, and as solitary as ever. But he was willing to play with me. He was happy to let me paint a sign-board for his shop. The idea was mine, and he took it seriously. He had a carpenter build a board of new wood; and on this, over some days, after priming and painting, I did the sign. He put it up over his shop door, and I thought it looked genuine, a real sign. I was amazed; it was the first sign-board I had ever done.

The time then came for me to go to England. I left Bogart in Carenage. And that was where he had continued to live in my memory, faintly, never a figure in the foreground: the man who had worked on a ship, then gone to Venezuela, sitting placidly ever after at his sewing machine, below my sign, in his little concrete house-and-shop.

That was Bogart's story, as I knew it. And – after all our migrations within Trinidad, after my own trip to England and my time at Oxford – that was all the story I had in mind when – after two failed attempts at novels – I sat at the typewriter in the freelances' room in the Langham Hotel, to try once more to be a writer. And luck was with me that afternoon. *Every morning when he got up Hat would sit on the banister of his back verandah and shout across, 'What happening there, Bogart?'* Luck was with me, because that first sentence was so direct, so uncluttered, so without complications, that it provoked the sentence that was to follow. *Bogart would turn in his bed and mumble softly, so that no one heard, 'What happening there, Hat?'*

The first sentence was true. The second was invention. But together – to me, the writer – they had done something extraordinary. Though they had left out everything – the setting, the historical time, the racial and social complexities of the people concerned – they had suggested it all; they had created the world of the street. And together, as sentences, words, they had set up a rhythm, a speed, which dictated all that was to follow.

The story developed a first-person narrator. And for the sake of speed, to avoid complications, to match the rhythm of what had gone before, this narrator could not be myself. My narrator lived alone with his mother in a house on the street. He had no father; he had no other family. So, very simply, all the crowd of my mother's extended family, as cumbersome in real life as it would have been to a writer, was abolished; and, again out of my wish to simplify, I had a narrator more in tune with the life of the street than I had been.

Bogart's tailoring business, with the sign-board I had done for him, I transferred from the Carenage side street to the Port of Spain servant room, and with it there came some hint of the silent companionableness I had found in Bogart at that later period. The servant room and the street – the houses, the pavements, the open yards, the American base at the end of the street – became like a stage set. Anyone might walk down the street; anyone might turn up in the servant room. It was enough – given the rhythm of the narrative and its accumulating suggestions of street life – for the narrator to say so. So Bogart could come and go, without fuss. When, in the story, he left the servant room for the first time, it took little – just the dropping of a few names – to establish the idea of the street as a kind of club.

So that afternoon in the Langham Hotel Port of Spain memories, disregarded until then, were simplified and transformed. The speed of the narrative – that was the speed of the writer. And everything that was later to look like considered literary devices came only from the anxiety of the writer. I wanted above all to take the story to the end. I feared that if I stopped too long anywhere I might lose faith in what I was doing, give up once more, and be left with nothing.

Speed dictated the solution of the mystery of Bogart. He wished to be free (of Hindu family conventions, but this wasn't stated in the story). He was without ambition, and had no skill; in spite of the sign-board, he was hardly a tailor. He was an unremarkable man, a man from the country, to whom mystery and the name of Bogart had been given by the street, which had its own city sense of drama. If Bogart spent whole afternoons in his servant room playing Patience, it was because he had no other way of passing the time. If, until he fell into the character of the film Bogart, he had no conversation, it was because he had little to say. The street saw him as sensual, lazy, cool. He was in fact passive. The emotional entanglements that called him away from the street were less than heroic. With women, Bogart – unlike most men of the street – had taken the easy way out. He was that flabby, emasculated thing, a bigamist. So, looking only for freedom, the Bogart of my story had ended up as a man on the run. It was only in the solitude of his servant room that he could be himself, at peace. It was only with the men and boys of the street that he could be a man.

The story was short, three thousand words, two foolscap sheets and a bit. I had – a conscious piece of magic that afternoon – set the typewriter at single space, to get as much as possible on the first sheet and also to create the effect of the printed page.

People were in and out of the freelances' room while I typed. Some would have dropped by at the BBC that afternoon for the company and the chat, and the off-chance of a commission by a producer for some little script. Some would have had work to do.

I suppose Ernest Eytle would have come in, to sit at the other typewriter and to peck, with many pauses, at the 'links' or even a 'piece' for the magazine programme. And Ernest's beautifully spoken words, crackling over the short wave that evening, would suggest a busy, alert man, deep in the metropolitan excitements of London, sparing a few minutes for his radio talk. He was a mulatto from British Guiana. He was dark-suited, fat and slow; when, some years later, I heard he had died, I was able mentally to transfer him, without any change, and without any feeling of shock, to a coffin. As much as broadcasting, Ernest liked the pub life around Broadcasting House. This sitting at the typewriter in the gloomy freelances' room was like an imposition; and Ernest, whenever he paused to think, would rub a heavy hand down his forehead to his eyebrows, which he pushed back the wrong way; and then, like a man brushing away cobwebs, he would appear to dust his cheek, his nose, his lips, and chin.

Having done that with Ernest, I should say that my own typing posture in those days was unusual. My shoulders were thrown back as far as they could go; my spine was arched. My knees were drawn right up; my shoes rested on the topmost struts of the chair, left side and right side. So, with my legs wide apart, I sat at the typewriter with something like a monkey crouch.

The freelances' room was like a club: chat, movement, the separate anxieties of young or youngish men below the passing fellowship of the room. That was the atmosphere I was writing in. That was the atmosphere I gave to Bogart's Port of Spain street. Partly for the sake of speed, and partly because my memory or imagination couldn't rise to it, I had given his servant room hardly any furniture: the Langham room itself was barely furnished. And I benefited from the fellowship of the room that afternoon. Without that fellowship, without the response of the three men who read the story, I might not have wanted to go on with what I had begun.

I passed the three typed sheets around.

John Stockbridge was English. He worked for many BBC programmes, domestic and overseas. Unlike the rest of us, he carried a briefcase; and that briefcase suggested method, steadiness, many commissions. At our first meeting in the freelances' room three or four months before, he hadn't been too friendly – he no doubt saw me as an Oxford man, untrained, stepping just like that into regular radio work, taking the bread out of the mouths of more experienced men. But then his attitude towards me had become one of schoolmasterly concern. He wanted to rescue me from what, with his English eyes, he saw as my self-neglect. He wanted me to make a better job of myself, to present myself well, to wear better clothes, and especially to get rid of my dingy working-class overcoat. (I knew nothing about clothes, but I had always thought the overcoat was wrong: it had been chosen for me, before I went up to Oxford, by the Maltese manageress of an Earl's Court boarding house.) Now, after he had read the story, John made a serious face and spoke a prodigious prophecy about my future as a writer. On such little evidence! But it was his way of finally accepting my ambition and my London life, and giving me a little blessing.

Andrew Salkey was a Jamaican. He worked in a night-club, was also trying to get started as a writer, and had just begun to do broadcasts, talks and readings. He compared learning to write with trying to wrap a whip around a rail; he thought I had begun to make the whip 'stick'. He detected, and made me take out, one or two early sentences where I had begun to lose faith in the material and had begun to ridicule, not the characters, but the idea that what I was doing was a real story.

The most wholehearted acceptance came from Gordon Woolford. He was from British Guiana. He came from a distinguished colonial family. He said he had some African ancestry, but it didn't show. Some deep trouble with his father had kept Gordon away from his family and committed him, after a privileged pre-war upbringing in Belgium and England, to a hard bohemian life in London. He was an unusually handsome man, in his mid-thirties. He had married a French girl, whom he had met when she was an assistant in one of the big London stores. That marriage had just broken up. Gordon was writing a novel about it, *On the Rocks*; it wasn't something he was going to finish. He changed jobs often; he loved writing; his favourite book – at least it was always with him during his drinking bouts – was *Scoop*.

Something in the Bogart story touched Gordon. When he finished reading the story he folded the sheets carefully; with a gesture as of acceptance he put the sheets in his inner jacket pocket; and then he led me out to the BBC club – he was not on the wagon that day. He read the story over again, and he made me read it with him, line by line, assessing the words and the tone: we might have been rehearsing a broadcast.

The manuscript still has his foldmarks and his wine stains.

During the writing of the Bogart story some memory – very vague, as if from a forgotten film – had come to me of the man who in 1938 or 1939, five years before Bogart, had lived in his servant room. He was a negro carpenter; the small sheltered space between the servant room and the back fence was at once his kitchen and workshop. I asked him one day what he was making. He said – wonderfully to the six-year-old child who had asked the question – that he was making 'the thing without a name'.

It was the carpenter's story that I settled down to write the next day in the freelances' room. I had little to go on. But I had a street, already peopled; I had an atmosphere; and I had a narrator. I stuck to the magic of the previous day: the non-rustle BBC paper, the typewriter set at single space. And I was conscious, with Gordon Woolford's help, of certain things I had stumbled on the previous day: never to let the words get too much in the way, to be fast, to add one concrete detail to another, and above all to keep the tone right.

I mentally set the servant room in another yard. *The only thing that Popo, who called himself a carpenter, ever built was the little galvanized-iron workshop under the mango tree at the back of his yard.* And then scattered memories, my narrator, the life of the street, and my own childhood sense (as a six-year-old coming suddenly to Port of Spain from the Hindu rigours of my grandmother's house in the country) of the intensity of the pleasures of people on the street, gave the carpenter a story. He was an idler, a happy man, a relisher of life; but then his wife left him.

Over the next few days the street grew. Its complexities didn't need to be pointed; they simply became apparent.

People who had only been names in one story got dialogue in the next, then became personalities; and old personalities became more familiar. Memory provided the material; city folklore as well, and city songs. An item from a London evening paper (about a postman throwing away his letters) was used. My narrator consumed material, and he seemed to be able to process every kind of material.

Even Gordon was written into the street. We were on the top of a bus one evening, going back from the BBC to Kilburn, the Irish working-class area where I lived in two rooms in the house of a BBC commissionaire. Gordon was talking of some early period of his life, some period of luxury and promise. Then he broke off, said, 'But that was a long time ago,' and looked down through the reflections of glass into the street. That went to my heart. Within a few days I was to run it into the memory of a negro ballad-maker, disturbed but very gentle, who had called at my grandmother's house in Port of Spain one day to sell copies of his poems, single printed sheets, and had told me a little of his life.

The stories became longer. They could no longer be written in a day. They were not always written in the free-lances' room. The technique became more conscious; it was not always possible to write fast. Beginnings, and the rhythms they established, didn't always come naturally; they had to be worked for. And then the material, which at one time had seemed inexhaustible, dried up. I had come to the end of what I could do with the street, in that particular way. *My mother said, 'You getting too wild in this place. I think is high time you leave.'* My narrator left the street, as I had left Trinidad five years before. And the excitement I had lived with for five or six weeks was over.

I had written a book, and I felt it to be real. That had been my ambition for years, and an urgent ambition for the past year. And I suppose that if the book had had some response outside the freelances' room I might have been a little more secure in my talent, and my later approach to writing would have been calmer; it is just possible.

But I knew only anxiety. The publisher that Andrew Salkey took the book to sent no reply for three months (the book remained unpublished for four years). And – by now one long year out of Oxford – I was trying to write another, and discovering that to have written a book was not to be a writer. Looking for a new book, a new narrative, episodes, I found myself as uncertain, and as pretending to be a writer, as I had been before I had written the story of Bogart.

To be a writer, I thought, was to have the conviction that one could go on. I didn't have that conviction. And even when the new book had been written I didn't think of myself as a writer. I thought I should wait until I had written three. And when, a year after writing the second, I had written the third, I thought I should wait until I had written six. On official forms I described myself as a 'broadcaster', thinking the word nondescript, suitable to someone from the freelances' room; until a BBC man, 'staff', told me it was boastful.

So I became 'writer'. Though to myself an unassuageable anxiety still attached to the word, and I was still, for its sake, practising magic. I never bought paper to write on. I preferred to use 'borrowed', non-rustle BBC paper; it seemed more casual, less likely to attract failure. I never numbered my pages, for fear of not getting to the end. (This drew the only comment Ernest Eytle made about my writing. Sitting idly at his typewriter one day in the freelances' room, he read some of my pages, apparently with goodwill. Then, weightily, he said, 'I'll tell you what you should do with this.' I waited. He said, 'You should number the pages. In case they get mixed up'.) And on the finished manuscripts of my first four books – half a million words – I never with my own hand typed or wrote my name. I always asked someone else to do that for me. Such anxiety; such ambition.

The ways of my fantasy, the process of creation, remained mysterious to me. For everything that was false or didn't work and had to be discarded, I felt that I alone was responsible. For everything that seemed right I felt I had only been a vessel. There was the recurring element of luck, or so it seemed to me. True, and saving, knowledge of my subject – beginning with Bogart's street – always seemed to come during the writing.

This element of luck isn't so mysterious to me now. As diarists and letter-writers repeatedly prove, any attempt at narrative can give value to an experience which might otherwise evaporate away. When I began to write about Bogart's street I began to sink into a tract of experience I hadn't before contemplated as a writer. This blindness might seem extraordinary in someone who wanted so much to be a writer. Half a writer's work, though, is the discovery of his subject. And a problem for me was that my life had been varied, full of upheavals and moves: from my grandmother's Hindu house in the country, still close to the rituals and social ways of village India; to Port of Spain, the negro and G.I. life of its streets, the other, ordered life of my colonial English school, which was called Queen's Royal College; and then Oxford, London and the freelances' room at the BBC.

Trying to make a beginning as a writer, I didn't know where to focus.

In England I was also a colonial. Out of the stresses of that, and out of my worship of the name of writer, I had without knowing it fallen into the error of thinking of writing as a kind of display. My very particularity – which was the subject sitting on my shoulder – had been encumbering me.

The English or French writer of my age had grown up in a world that was more or less explained. He wrote against a background of knowledge. I couldn't be a writer in the same way, because to be a colonial, as I was, was to be spared knowledge. It was to live in an intellectually restricted world; it was to accept those restrictions. And the restrictions could become attractive.

Every morning when he got up Hat would sit on the banister of his back verandah and shout across, 'What happening there, Bogart?' That was a good place to begin. But I couldn't stay there. My anxiety constantly to prove myself as a writer, the need to write another book and then another, led me away.

There was much in that call of 'Bogart!' that had to be examined. It was spoken by a Port of Spain Indian, a descendant of nineteenth-century indentured immigrants from South India; and Bogart was linked in a special Hindu way with my mother's family. So there was a migration from India to be considered, a migration within the British Empire. There was my Hindu family, with its fading memories of India; there was India itself. And there was Trinidad, with its past of slavery, its mixed population, its racial antagonisms and its changing political life; once part of Venezuela and the Spanish Empire, now English-speaking, with the American base and an open-air cinema at the end of Bogart's street. And just across the Gulf of Paria was Venezuela, the sixteenth-century land of El Dorado, now a country of dictators, but drawing Bogart out of his servant room with its promise of Spanish sexual adventure and the promise of a job in its oilfields.

And there was my own presence in England, writing: the career wasn't possible in Trinidad, a small, mainly agricultural colony: my vision of the world couldn't exclude that important fact.

So step by step, book by book, though seeking each time only to write another book, I eased myself into knowledge. To write was to learn. Beginning a book, I always felt I was in possession of all the facts about myself; at the end I was always surprised. The book before always turned out to have been written by a man with incomplete knowledge. And the very first, the one begun in the freelances' room, seemed to have been written by an innocent, a man at the beginning of knowledge both about himself and the writing career that had been his ambition from childhood.

2

The ambition to be a writer was given me by my father. He was a journalist for much of his working life. This was an unusual occupation for a Trinidad Indian of his generation. My father was born in 1906. At that time the Indians of Trinidad were a separate community, mainly rural and Hindi-speaking, attached to the sugar estates of central and southern

Trinidad. Many of the Indians of 1906 had been born in India and had come out to Trinidad as indentured labourers on five-year contracts. This form of Indian contract labour within the British Empire ended, as a result of nationalist agitation in India, only in 1917.

In 1929 my father began contributing occasional articles on Indian topics to the *Trinidad Guardian*. In 1932, when I was born, he had become the *Guardian* staff correspondent in the little market town of Chaguanas. Chaguanas was in the heart of the sugar area and the Indian area of Trinidad. It was where my mother's family was established. Contract labour was far behind them; they were big landowners.

Two years or so after I was born my father left the *Guardian*, for reasons that were never clear to me. For some years he did odd jobs here and there, now attached to my mother's family, now going back to the protection of an uncle by marriage, a rich man, founder and part owner of the biggest bus company in the island. Poor himself, with close relations who were still agricultural labourers, my father dangled all his life in a half-dependence and half-esteem between these two powerful families.

In 1938 my father was taken on by the *Guardian* again, this time as a city reporter. And we – my father, my mother and their five children, our own little nucleus within my mother's extended family – moved to Port of Spain, to the house owned by my mother's mother. That was when I was introduced to the life of the street (and the mystery of the negro carpenter in the servant room, making 'the thing without a name'). That was also when I got to know my father.

I had lived before then (at least in my own memory) in my mother's family house in Chaguanas. I knew I had a father, but I also knew and accepted that – like the fathers of others of my cousins – he was not present. There was a gift one year of a very small book of English poetry; there was a gift another time of a toy set of carpenter's tools. But the man himself remained vague.

He must have been in the house, though; because in the subsidiary two-storey wooden house at the back of the main building there were – on the inner wall of the upstairs verandah – jumbled ghostly impressions of banners or posters he had painted for someone in my mother's family who had fought a local election. The cotton banners had been stretched on the verandah wall; the beautiful oil paint, mainly red, had soaked through, disfiguring (or simply adding to) the flowered designs my mother's father (now dead) had had painted on the lower part of the verandah wall. The glory, of the election and my father's banners, belonged to the past; I accepted that.

My mother's family house in Chaguanas was a well-known local 'big house'. It was built in the North Indian style. It had balustraded roof terraces, and the main terrace was decorated at either end with a statue of a rampant lion. I didn't like or dislike living there; it was all I knew. But I liked the move to Port of Spain, to the emptier house, and the pleasures and sights of the city: the squares, the gardens, the children's playground, the street lights, the ships in the harbour.

There was no American base at the end of the street. The land, still hardly with a name, known only as Docksite, had just been reclaimed, and the grey mud dredged up from the harbour was still drying out, making wonderful patterns as it crusted and cracked. After the shut-in compound life of the house in Chaguanas, I liked living on a city street. I liked looking at other people, other families. I liked the way things looked. In the morning the shadows of houses and trees fell on the pavement opposite; in the afternoon our pavement was in shadow. And I liked the municipal order of each day: the early-morning cleaning of the streets, with the hydrants turned on to flood the green-slimed gutters with fresh water; the later collection of refuse; the passing in mid-morning of the ice-cart.

Our house stood on high concrete pillars. The newspaper man threw the *Guardian* as high as he could up the concrete front steps. This delivery of a paper was one of the novelties of my Port of Spain life. And I also knew that, because my father worked for the *Guardian*, the paper was delivered free. So I had a feeling of privilege, a double sense of drama. And just as I had inherited or been given a feeling for lettering, so now I began to be given ambitions connected with the printed word. But these ambitions were twisted. They were not connected with the simple reporting that my father was doing for the *Guardian* at that time – he didn't like what he was doing. The ambitions were connected with what my father had done for the *Guardian* long before, in that past out of which he had so suddenly appeared to me.

My father had a bookcase-and-desk. It was a bulky piece of furniture, stained dark red and varnished, with glass doors to the three bookshelves, and a lipped, sloping, hinged lid to the desk. It was made from pine and packing crates (the raw, unstained side panel of one drawer was stencilled *Stow away from boilers*). It was part of the furniture my father had brought from where he had been living in the country. I was introduced to this furniture in Port of Spain, recognized it as my father's and therefore mine, and got to like each piece; in my grandmother's house in Chaguanas nothing had belonged to me.

Below the sloping lid of the desk, and in the square, long drawers, were my father's records: old papers, where silver fish squirmed and mice sometimes nested, with their pink young – to be thrown out into the yard for chickens to peck at. My father liked to keep documents. There were letters from a London writing school, letters from the *Guardian*. I read them all, many times, and always with pleasure, relishing them as things from the past; though the raised letter-heads meant more to me than the letters. There was a passport with my father's picture – a British passport, for someone from the colony of Trinidad and Tobago; this passport had never been used. And there was a big ledger in which my father had pasted his early writings for the *Guardian*. It was an estate wages ledger; the newspaper cuttings had been pasted over the names of the labourers and the wages they had been paid week by week.

This ledger became one of the books of my childhood. It was there, in the old-fashioned *Guardian* type and lay-out – and not in the paper that fell on the front steps every morning, sometimes while it was still dark – that I got to love the idea of newspapers and the idea of print.

I saw my father's name in print, in the two spellings, Naipal and Naipaul. I saw the pen-names that in those glorious days he had sometimes also used: Paul Nye, Paul Prye. He had written a lot, and I had no trouble understanding that the *Guardian* had been a better paper then. The Chaguanas that my father had written about was more full of excitement and stories than the Chaguanas I had known. The place seemed to have degenerated, with the paper.

My father had written about village feuds, family vendettas, murders, bitter election battles. (And how satisfying to see, in print, the names of those relations of my mother's whose ghostly election banners, from a subsequent election, I had seen on the verandah wall of my mother's family house!) My father had written about strange characters. Like the negro 'hermit': once rich and pleasure-seeking, now penniless and living alone with a dog in a hut in the swamp-lands. The *Guardian* called my father's hermit Robinson Crusoe. Then, true to his new name, this Crusoe decided to go to Tobago, Crusoe's island; he intended to walk there; and, fittingly, there was no more about him. There was the negro woman of 112 who said she remembered the days of slavery when 'negroes were lashed to poles and flogged'. That didn't mean much; but the words (which made one of the headlines) stuck, because I didn't know that particular use of 'lash'.

My father had his own adventures. Once, on a rainy night, and far from home, his motorcycle skidded off the road and for some reason he had to spend the night up a tree. Was that true? I don't remember what my father said, but I understood that the story was exaggerated.

It didn't matter. I read the stories as stories; they were written by my father; I went back to them as to memorials of a heroic time I had missed. There was something about the ledger I noticed but never asked about, accepting it as a fact about the ledger: the clippings stopped quite suddenly; at least a third of the book remained unused.

In the *Guardian* that came to the house every day my father's name didn't appear. The style of the paper had changed; the reporting was all anonymous. The paper was part of the drama of the early morning, but I was interested in it only as a printed object. I didn't think to look for what my father had written.

The fact was I was too young for newspapers. I was old enough only for stories. The ledger in the desk was like a personal story. In it the ideas of 'once upon a time' and my father's writing life in old Chaguanas came together and penetrated my imagination, together with Charles Kingsley's story of Perseus (a baby cast out to sea, a mother enslaved), which was the first story my father read to me; the early chapters of *Oliver Twist*; Mr Murdstone from *David Copperfield*; Mr Squeers. All this my father introduced me to. All this was added to my discovery of Port of Spain and the life of our street. It was the richest and most serene time of my childhood.

It didn't last long. It lasted perhaps for two years. My mother's mother decided to leave Chaguanas. She bought a cocoa estate of 350 acres in the hills to the north-west of Port of Spain, and it was decided – by the people in the family who decided on such matters – that the whole family, or all its dependent branches, should move there. My mother was willing enough to be with her family again. The rest of us were not so willing. But we had to go. We had to leave the house in Port of Spain. After the quiet and order of our two years as a separate unit we were returned to the hubbub of the extended family and our scattered nonentity within it.

The intention was good, even romantic. It was that the family should together work the rich and beautiful estate. It was more the idea of the commune than a continuation of the extended family life of Chaguanas, where most people had their own land and houses and used the family house as a centre. Here we all lived in the estate house. It was a big house, but it wasn't big enough; and the idea of communal labour turned out to be little more than the exaction of labour from the helpless.

In Chaguanas the family had been at the centre of a whole network of Hindu reverences. People were always coming to the Chaguanas house to pay their respects, to issue invitations, or to bring gifts of food. Here we were alone. Unsupported by that Chaguanas world, with no one outside to instruct us in our obligations, even to ourselves, our own internal reverences began to go; our Hindu system began to fail.

There were desperate quarrels. Animosities and alliances shifted all the time; people had constantly to be looked at in new ways. Nothing was stable. Food was short; transport to Port of Spain difficult. I didn't see my father for days. His nerves deteriorated. He had been given one of the servant rooms (we children slept anywhere). In that room one Sunday evening, in a great rage, he threw a glass of hot milk. It cut me above my right eye; my eyebrow still shows the scar.

After two years we moved back to the house in Port of Spain, but only to some rooms in it. There was a period of calm, especially after my father got a job with the government and left the *Guardian*. But we were under pressure. More and more people from my mother's family were coming to Port of Spain, and we were squeezed into less and less space. The street itself had changed. On the reclaimed area of Docksite there was the American base; and at least one of the houses or yards had become a kind of brothel ground.

Disorder within, disorder without. Only my school life

was ordered; anything that had happened there I could date at once. But my family life – my life at home or my life in the house, in the street – was jumbled, without sequence. The sequence I have given it here has come to me only with the writing of this piece. And that is why I am not sure whether it was before the upheaval of our move or after our return to Port of Spain that I became aware of my father writing stories.

In one of the drawers of the desk there was a typescript – on *Guardian* 'copy' paper – of a story called 'White Man's Way'. It was an old story and it didn't mean much to me. A white overseer on a horse, a girl in a cane-field: I cannot remember what happened. I was at sea with this kind of story. For all my reputation in the house as a reader of books – and my interest in books and magazines as printed objects was genuine – there was an element of pretence, a carry-over from the schoolroom, in much of the reading I did on my own. It was easier for me to take an interest in what my father read to me. And my father never read this story aloud to me.

I remember that in the story there was a phrase about the girl's breasts below her bodice; and I suppose that my father had grafted his sexual yearnings on to an English or American magazine-style tropical story. In the desk, hoarded with his other papers, there was a stack of these magazines, often looked at by me, never really read. My father had done or partly done a correspondence course with a London writing school before the war – some of the letters were in the desk. The school had recommended a study of the 'market'. These magazines were the market.

But 'White Man's Way' was in the past. The stories my father now began to write were aimed at no market. He wrote in fits and starts. He wrote in bed, with a pencil. He wrote slowly, with great patience; he could write the same paragraph over and over again. Liable to stomach pains, and just as liable to depressions (his calls then for 'the Epictetus' or 'the Marcus Aurelius', books of comfort, were like calls for his stomach medicine), my father became calm before and during his writing moods.

He didn't write a great deal. He wrote one long story and four or five shorter stories. In the shorter pieces my father, moving far from my mother's family and the family of his uncle by marriage, recreated his own background. The people he wrote about were poor, but that wasn't the point. These stories celebrated Indian village life, and the Hindu rituals that gave grace and completeness to that life. They also celebrated elemental things, the order of the working day, the labour of the rice-fields, the lighting of the cooking fire in the half-walled gallery of a thatched hut, the preparation and eating of food. There was very little 'story' in these stories. But to me they gave a beauty (which in a corner of my mind still endures, like a fantasy of home) to the Indian village life I had never known. And when we went to the country to visit my father's own relations, who were the characters in these stories, it was like a fairytale come to life.

The long story was quite different. It was comic; yet it dealt with cruelty. It was the story of an Indian village thug. He is taken out of school at fourteen in order to be married: a boy of high caste, as the protagonist is, should be married before his whiskers grow. In the alien, Presbyterian school the boy is momentarily abashed by the idea of his early marriage; at home he is proud of the manhood this marriage confers. He terrorizes and beats his wife: strong men should beat their wives. Secure in his own eyes as a brahmin and the son of a landowner, he disdains work and seeks glory. He uses his father's money and authority to establish and lead a village stick-fighting group, though he himself has no skill in that exacting and elegant martial art. None of this is done for gain; it is all done for glory, a caste idea of manhood, a wish for battle, a wish to be a leader. The quality of the ambition is high; the village setting is petty. The would-be caste chieftain ends in the alien police courts as an uneducated country criminal, speaking broken English.

I was involved in the slow making of this story from the beginning to the end. Every new bit was read out to me, every little variation; and I read every new typescript my father made as the story grew. It was the greatest imaginative experience of my childhood. I knew the story by heart, yet always loved to read it or hear it, feeling a thrill at every familiar turn, ready for all the varied emotions. Growing up within my extended family, knowing nothing else, or looking at everything else from the outside, I had no social sense, no sense of other societies; and as a result, reading (mainly English books) was difficult for me. I couldn't enter worlds that were not like mine. I could get on only with the broadest kind of story, the fairytale. The world of this story of my father's was something I knew. To the pastoral beauty of his other stories it added cruelty, and comedy that made the cruelty just bearable. It was my private epic.

With the encouragement, and possibly the help, of my mother's elder brother, my father printed the stories. That was another excitement. And then somehow, without any discussion that I remember, it seemed to be settled, in my mind as well as my father's, that I was to be a writer.

On the American base at the end of the street the flag was raised every morning and lowered every evening; the bugle sounded twice a day. The street was full of Americans, very neat in their shiny starched uniforms. At night the sound-track of the open-air American cinema thundered away. The man in the yard next door slaughtered a goat in his back gallery every Sunday morning and hung the red carcase up, selling pieces. This slaughtering of the goat was a boisterous business; the man next door, to attract customers, made it appear like a celebration of the holiday. And every morning he called out to the man in the servant room in our yard: 'Bogart!' Fantasy calling to fantasy on our street. And in the two rooms to which we had been reduced, our fantasy was dizzier. I was eleven; I had given no sign of talent; but I was to be a writer.

On the window frame beside his bed, where he did his writing, my father had hung a framed picture of O. Henry, cut out from the jacket of the Hodder and Stoughton uniform edition. 'O. Henry, the greatest short story writer the world has ever known.' All that I know of this writer to this day are the three stories my father read to me. One was 'The Gift of the Magi', a story of two poor lovers who, to buy gifts for each other, make sacrifices that render the gifts useless. The second story (as I remember it) was about a tramp who decides in a dream to reform and then wakes up to find a policeman about to arrest him. The third story – about a condemned man waiting to be electrocuted – was unfinished; O. Henry died while writing it. That unfinished story made an impression on me, as did the story of O. Henry's own death. He had asked for the light to be kept on and had spoken a line from a popular song: 'I don't want to go home in the dark.'

Poverty, cheated hopes, and death: those were the associations of the framed picture beside my father's bed. From the earliest stories and bits of stories my father had read to me, before the upheaval of the move, I had arrived at the conviction – the conviction that is at the root of so much human anguish and passion, and corrupts so many lives – that there was justice in the world. The wish to be a writer was a development of that. To be a writer as O. Henry was, to die in mid-sentence, was to triumph over darkness. And like a wild religious faith that hardens in adversity, this wish to be a writer, this refusal to be extinguished, this wish to seek at some future time for justice, strengthened as our conditions grew worse in the house on the street.

Our last two years in that house – our last two years in the extended family – were very bad indeed. At the end of 1946, when I was fourteen, my father managed to buy his own house. By that time my childhood was over; I was fully made.

The wish to be a writer didn't go with a wish or a need actually to write. It went only with the idea I had been given of the writer, a fantasy of nobility. It was something that lay ahead, and outside the life I knew – far from family and clan, city, colony, *Trinidad Guardian*, negroes.

In 1948 I won a Trinidad government scholarship. These scholarships were meant to give a man a profession and they could last for seven years. I decided to use mine to do English at Oxford. I didn't want the degree; I wanted only to get away; and I thought that in my three or four scholarship years at Oxford my talent would somehow be revealed, and the books would start writing themselves.

My father had written little. I was aware now of the trouble he had finding things to write about. He had read little, was only a dipper – I never knew him to read a book through. His idea of the writer – as a person triumphant and detached – was a private composite of O. Henry, Warwick Deeping, Marie Corelli (of the *Sorrows of Satan*), Charles Dickens, Somerset Maugham, and J. R. Ackerley (of *Hindoo Holiday*). My own reading was not much better. My inability to understand other societies made nonsense of the Huxley and D. H. Lawrence and the Evelyn Waugh I tried to read, and even of the Stendhal I had read at school. And I had written scarcely at all. If the O. Henry trick ending stood in the way of my father's writing, Huxley and Lawrence and Waugh made me feel I had no material. But it had been settled that I was to be a writer. That was the career I was travelling to.

I left Trinidad in 1950. It was five years later, in the BBC freelances' room, that I thought to write of the shout of 'Bogart!' That shout came from a tormented time. But that was not how I remembered it. My family circumstances had been too confused; I preferred not to focus on them; in my mind they had no sequence. My narrator, recording the life of his street, was as serene as I had been when we had first moved to Port of Spain with my father.

At the end of the book my narrator left his street. *I left them all and walked briskly towards the aeroplane, not looking back, looking only at my shadow before me, a dancing dwarf on the tarmac.* That line, the last in the book, wrote itself. It held memories of the twelve years, no more, I had spent with my father. The movement of the shadows of trees and houses across the street – more dramatic to me than the amorphous shadows of Chaguanas – was one of the first things I had noticed in Port of Spain. And it was with that sudden churlishness, a sudden access of my own hysteria, that I had left my father in 1950, not looking back. I wish I had. I might have taken away, and might still possess, some picture of him on that day. He died miserably – back at the tormenting *Guardian* – three years later.

To become a writer, that noble thing, I had thought it necessary to leave. Actually to write, it was necessary to go back. It was the beginning of self-knowledge.

3

In 1977, after twenty-seven years, I saw Bogart again. He hadn't been important in our family; he had always liked to hide; and for more than twenty years I had had no news of him. I had grown to think of him as a vanished person, one of the many I had left behind for good when I left Trinidad.

Then I discovered that he too had left Trinidad, and not long after I had left, not long after I had done the sign for his tailoring shop in Carenage. He had gone to Venezuela. There he had been for all this time. As a child, considering his disappearances and returns, I had divined his dreams (because they were also partly mine) of sensual fulfilment in another land and another language. And then, in the story I had devised for him in one afternoon, I had cruelly made him a bigamist. He had been part of my luck as a writer. My ignorance of his true story had been part of that luck. I had been free to simplify and work fast.

I was going now, in 1977, to spend some weeks in Venezuela. And when I passed through Trinidad I tried to get Bogart's address. That wasn't easy. He still apparently caused embarrassment to his close relations. And then there was some confusion about the address itself. The first address I was given was in the oil town of Maracaibo, in the west. The second was on the former pearl island of Margarita, three or four hundred miles to the east, on the Caribbean coast. That was like the old Bogart: a man on the move. He seemed, from this second address, to be in business in Margarita, as 'international traders' or an 'international trading corporation' or an 'import-export corporation'.

Venezuela was rich, with its oil. Trinidad was now also rich, with the oil that had been discovered off-shore. But when I was a child Trinidad was poor, even with the American bases; and Venezuela was a place to which people like Bogart tried to go.

Many went illegally. In a fishing boat it was a passage of a few hours, no more than a drift with the strong current, across the southern mouth of the Gulf of Paria. In the mixed population of the villages in the Orinoco delta, far from authority, Trinidadians who were protected could pass. Some acquired Venezuelan birth certificates; so it happened that men whose grandfathers had come from India sank into the personalities, randomly issued by the migration brokers, of Spanish mulattoes named Morales or Garcia or Ybarra.

These men didn't go only for the money. They went for the adventure. Venezuela was the Spanish language, South America: a continent. Trinidad was small, an island, a British colony. The maps in our geography books, concentrating on British islands in the Caribbean, seemed to stress our smallness and isolation. In the map of Trinidad, the map which I grew to carry in my head, Venezuela was an unexplained little peninsula in the top left-hand corner.

True knowledge of geography, and with it a sense of historical wonder, began to come sixteen years after I had left Trinidad, when for two years I worked on a history of the region. For those two years – reading in the British Museum, the Public Record Office, the London Library – I lived with the documents of our region, seeking to detach the region from big historical 'over-views', trying only to understand how my corner of the New World, once indeed new, and capable of developing in any number of ways, had become the place it was.

I saw the Gulf of Paria with the eyes of the earliest explorers and officials: I saw it as an aboriginal Indian lake, busy with canoes, sometimes of war. To those Indians, crossing easily back and forth, Trinidad was Venezuela in small. There was a mighty Caroni river in Venezuela; there was a small Caroni, a stream, in Trinidad. There was a Chaguaramas in Trinidad; there was a Chaguaramas in Venezuela.

Trinidad sat in the mouth of the Orinoco, beyond the 'drowned lands' of the delta that Sir Walter Ralegh saw: now a refuge for people from the mainland, now a base for attack. To the Spaniards Trinidad guarded the river that led to El Dorado. When that fantasy faded, all that province of El Dorado – Trinidad and Guiana and the drowned lands – was left to bush. But the Indians were ground down. One day in the British Museum I found out about the name of my birthplace, Chaguanas.

Ralegh's last, lunatic raid on 'El Dorado' had taken place in 1617. Eight years later the Spaniards were settling accounts with the local Indians. On 12 October 1625 the King of Spain wrote to the Governor of Trinidad: 'I asked you to give me some information about a certain nation of Indians called Chaguanes, who you say are above one thousand and of such bad disposition that it was they who led the English when they captured the town. Their crime hasn't been punished because forces were not available for this purpose and because the Indians acknowledge no master save their own will. You have decided to give them a punishment. Follow the rules I have given you; and let me know how you get on.'

I felt that I was the first person since the seventeenth century to whom that document had spoken so directly. A small tribe, one among hundreds – they had left behind only their name. The Chaguanas I knew was an Indian country town, Indian of India. Hindi-speaking Indians had simplified the name into a Hindu caste name, Chauhan. It had its Hindu districts and its Muslim districts; it had the religious and caste rivalries of India. It was where my mother's father had bought many acres of cane-land and rice-land and where he had built his Indian-style house. It was also where, from a reading of my father's stories of village life, I had set my fantasy of home, my fantasy of things as they were at the very beginning: the ritualized day, fields and huts, the mango tree in the yard, the simple flowers, the lighting of fires in the evening.

Trinidad I knew too well. It was, profoundly, part of my past. That past lay over the older past; and I couldn't, when I was in Trinidad again, see it as the setting of the aboriginal history I knew and had written about. But I had written about Venezuela and its waters without having seen them. The historical Venezuela – as it existed in my imagination – was vivid to me. And, when I went on to Venezuela from Trinidad in 1977, all that I saw as the aeroplane tilted away from the island was fresh and hallowed, the land and sea of the earliest travellers: the great froth-fringed stain of the Orinoco on the Gulf, the more local, muddier stains of small rivers from the Paria Peninsula (the unexplained peninsula in the left-hand corner of the school map of Trinidad). In 1604, sixteen years after the defeat of the Spanish Armada he had led against England, the Duke of Medina Sidonia had been sent here by the King of Spain, to report on the best way of defending this coast and especially the salt-pans of Araya (into which the Paria Peninsula ran, after 150 miles). Such a task! (And, when I got to know it later, such a desolation still, Araya, on its Caribbean coast: thorn trees and cactus in a hummocked red desert beside the murky sea, life only in the long, slack waves, the vultures in the sky, and the pelicans, all beak and belly and wings, undisturbed on their rock-perches.)

To land at La Guaira airport, on the Venezuelan coast, was to come down to a different country. Scores of bulldozers were levelling the red earth to extend the airport. There were yachts in the marina beside the big resort hotel. The highway that led to Caracas in its inland valley had for stretches been tunnelled through the mountains.

Venezuela was rich. But in its oil economy many of its people were superfluous. The restaurants of the capital were Spanish or Italian, the hotels American. The technicians in the industrial towns that were being built in the interior were European; people spoke of a second Spanish conquest. Oil money – derived from foreign machines, foreign markets – fed a real-estate boom in the towns. Agriculture was neglected; it was like something from the poor past. The descendants of the people who had been brought in long ago to restock the Indian land, to work the plantations, were no longer needed. Still pure negro in the cocoa areas (fragrant with the scent of vanilla), old mulatto mixtures elsewhere, they had been abandoned with the plantations. And to travel out to the countryside was to see – on a continental scale – a kind of peasant dereliction that had vanished from Trinidad: shacks and a few fruit trees in small yards, rough little roadside stalls offering fruit from the yards.

It was in a setting like that, on the island of Margarita, in a setting close to what he had known in Trinidad, when I had painted the sign for him at Carenage, that I found Bogart.

Columbus had given Margarita its name, 'the pearl'. It was across the sea from Araya, and early maps magnified its size. Pearl diving had used up the Indians fast; and there were no pearls now. Margarita lived as a resort island and a duty-free zone: Venezuelans flew over from the mainland to shop. Half the island was desert, as red as Araya; half was green.

Bogart was in the green part. I had imagined, because I had understood he was in the import-export business, that he would be in one of the little towns. He was in a village, far from town or beach. It took some finding – and then suddenly in mid-afternoon, a glaring, shadowless time, in a dusty rural lane, very local, with no sign of resort life or duty-free activity, I was there: little houses, corrugated-iron shacks, open yards, fruit trees growing out of blackened, trampled earth, their promise of a little bounty adding (to me, who had known such places as a child) to the feeling of dirt and poverty and empty days.

Bogart's shop was a little concrete-walled building. Without the big sign painted on the wall I might have missed it. The two brown doors of the shop were closed. The side gate to the yard was closed. In the open yard to one side, in an unwalled shed attached as extra living space to an old, two-roomed wooden house, a bent old woman, not white, not brown, was taking her ease on a wooden bench: kerchiefed, long-skirted, too old now for a siesta, existing at that moment only in a daze of heat, dullness and old age: pans and plates on a table beside her, potted plants on the ground.

I banged for a long time on Bogart's side gate. At last it opened: a mulatto girl of fifteen or sixteen or seventeen held it open. The old woman next door was swaddled in her long skirt; the light, loose frock of this girl was like the merest covering over her hard little body, and she was in slippers, someone at ease, someone at home. She was pale brown, well-fed, with an oval face.

The questioning in her eyes vanished when she saw the taxi in the road. Her demeanour moderated, but only slightly, into that of the servant. She let me in without a word and then seemed to stand behind me. So that any idea that she might be Bogart's daughter left me, and I thought of her as one of the un-needed, one of the many thousands littered in peasant yards and cast out into the wilderness of Venezuela.

The dirt yard over which the girl had walked in slippers was smooth and swept. At the back of the shop, and at a right angle to it, was a row of two or three rooms with a wide verandah all the way down. From one of these rooms Bogart soon appeared, dressing fast: I had interrupted his siesta. So that, though he was now a man of sixty or more, he was as I had remembered him: heavy-lidded, sleepy. He used to have a smoothness of skin and softness of body that suggested he might become fat. He still had the skin and the softness, but he hadn't grown any fatter.

He called me by the name used by my family. I had trouble with his. I had grown up calling him by the Hindi word for a maternal uncle. That didn't seem suitable now; but I couldn't call him by his name either. In that moment of greeting and mutual embarrassment the girl disappeared.

He had got my telegram, he said; and he had sent a telegram in reply – but I hadn't got that. He didn't ask me into any of the back rooms or even the verandah. He opened up the back door of the shop. He seated me facing the dark shop – stocked mainly with cloth. He sat facing the bright yard. Even after twenty-seven years, I clearly wasn't to stay long.

His voice was gruffer, but there was no trace of Venezuela in his English accent. The light from the yard showed his puffy, sagging cheeks and the black interstices of his teeth. That mouthful of apparently rotten teeth weakened his whole face and gave a touch of inanity to his smile.

His subject, after routine family inquiries, was himself. He never asked what I had done with my life, or even what I was doing in Venezuela. Like many people who live in small or retarded communities, he had little curiosity. His own life was his only story. But that was what I wanted to hear.

When he was a young man, during the war, he said, he had made a trip to Venezuela. He had become involved with a local woman. To his great alarm, she had had a child for him.

Bogart said, 'But you knew that.'

I didn't know it. Nothing had been said about Bogart's misadventure. Our family kept its secrets well.

For some years after that he had divided his time between Trinidad and Venezuela, freedom and the woman. Finally –

since there was no job for him in Trinidad – he had settled in Venezuela. He had got a job with an oil company, and there he had stayed. That was the let-down for me: that Bogart, the adventurer, with his own idea of the Spanish Main, should have lived a life of routine for twenty-five years. He would still have been in that job, he said, if it hadn't been for a malevolent negro. The negro, raised to a little authority and rendered vicious, tormented him. In the end Bogart left the job, with a reduced gratuity. He was glad to leave. That life hadn't really been satisfactory, he said. The woman hadn't been satisfactory. His children had been a disappointment; they were not bright.

Not bright! This judgment, from Bogart! It was astonishing that he could go back to an old way of thinking, that he could create this picture of his Venezuelan family as mulatto nondescripts. But he was also saying, obliquely, that he had left his wife and children on the mainland and had come to the island to make a fresh start. That explained the confusion about the two addresses. It also explained the demeanour of the mulatto girl, who wasn't allowed to appear again.

He had been part of my luck as a writer; his simplicity had been part of that luck. Even as a child, I had divined his impulses. He wasn't a bigamist, as I had made him in my story. But he had been caught by the senses; and now in old age he was seeking again the liberation he had been looking for when he had come to our street in Port of Spain.

But he was old now. He had begun to have some sense of life as an illusion, and his thoughts were turning to higher things – they had begun to turn that way when he was having trouble with the negro. He didn't know how to pray, he said.

He had never paid attention to the pundits – he spoke apologetically, addressing me as someone whose family was full of pundits. But every morning, before he ate, he bathed and sat cross-legged and for half an hour he took the name of Rama – Rama, the Indo-Aryan epic hero, the embodiment of virtue, God himself, the name Gandhi had spoken twice, after he had been shot.

After telling his story, old family graces seemed to return to Bogart. He hadn't offered hospitality; now he offered anything in his shop. Shoddy goods, for the local market. I took a scarf, synthetic, lightweight material. And then it was close to opening time, and time for me to go.

Outside, I studied the lettering on the shop wall. The paint was new; the sign-writer's rules and pencil outlines were still visible. Perhaps the sign I had done for him twenty-seven or twenty-eight years before had given him the taste for signs. This one was very big. *Grandes Rebajas! Aprovéchese!* 'Big Reductions! Don't Miss Them!' The Spanish language: no romance in these workaday words now.

He had lived the life of freedom, and it had taken him back almost to where he had been in the beginning. But though he appeared not to know it, the Hindu family life he had wanted to escape from – the life of our extended family, our clan – had distintegrated in Trinidad. The family Bogart had known in my grandmother's house in Port of Spain – neutered men, oppressed and cantankerous women, uneducated children – had scattered, and changed. To everyone there had come the wish to break away; and the disintegration of our private Hindu world – in all, we were fifty cousins – had released energy in people who might otherwise have remained passive. Many of my cousins, starting late, acquired professions, wealth; some migrated to more demanding lands.

For all its physical wretchedness and internal tensions, the life of the clan had given us all a start. It had given us a caste certainty, a high sense of the self. Bogart had escaped too soon; still passive, he had settled for nullity. Now, discovering his desolation, he was turning to religion, something that he thought was truly his own. He had only memories to guide him. His memories were not of sacred books and texts, but rituals, forms. So he could think only of bathing in the mornings, sitting in a certain posture, and speaking the name of Rama. It was less a wish for religion and old ritual, less a wish for the old life than a wish, in the emptiness of his Venezuela, for the consolation of hallowed ways.

Thinking of him, I remembered something I had seen eight years before in Belize, south of Yucatán, near the great ancient Mayan site of Altun Ha. The site, a complex of temples spread over four square miles, had been abandoned some centuries before the coming of the Spaniards. The steep-stepped temples had become forested hills; and in the forest beside the main road there were still many unexcavated small hills, hard to see unless you were looking for them.

The priests of Altun Ha had been killed perhaps a thousand years before; there might have been a peasant uprising. That was the theory of the Canadian archaeologist who was living on the site in a tent marked with the name of his university. Not far away, on the edge of a government camp beside a stream, a Mayan peasant was building a hut. He had put up the pillars – trimmed tree-branches – and the roof-frame. Now he was marking out the boundary of his plot. It was an act that called for some ritual, and the man was walking along the boundary, swinging smoking copal in a wicker censer, and muttering. He was making up his own incantation. The words were gibberish.

When I got back to Caracas I found the telegram Bogart said he had sent me. *Sorry but your visit not possible now Am in and out all the time these days It's me alone here in Margarita.*

4

The local history I studied at school was not interesting. It offered so little. It was like the maps in the geography books that stressed the islands and virtually did away with the contintent. We were a small part of somebody else's 'overview': we were part first of the Spanish story, then of the British story. Perhaps the school histories could be written in no other way. We were, after all, a small agricultural colony; and we couldn't say we had done much. (The current 'revolutionary' or Africanist overview is not an improvement: it is no more than the old imperialist attitude turned inside out.) To discover the wonder of our situation as children of the New World we had to look into ourselves; and to someone from my kind of Hindu background that wasn't easy.

I grew up with two ideas of history, almost two ideas of time. There was history with dates. That kind of history affected people and places abroad, and my range was wide: ancient Rome (the study of which, during my last two years at Queen's Royal College in Port of Spain, was the most awakening part of my formal education); nineteenth-century England; the nationalist movement in India.

But Chaguanas, where I was born, in an Indian-style house

my grandfather had built, had no dates. If I read in a book
that Gandhi had made his first call for civil disobedience in
India in 1919, that date seemed recent. But 1919, in Chaguanas, in the life of the Indian community, was almost un-
imaginable. It was a time beyond recall, mythical. About our
family, the migration of our ancestors from India, I knew
only what I knew or what I was told. Beyond (and sometimes
even within) people's memories was undated time, historical
darkness. Out of that darkness (extending to place as well as
to time) we had all come. The India where Gandhi and Nehru
and the others operated was historical and real. The India
from which we had come was impossibly remote, almost as
imaginary as the land of the *Ramayana*, our Hindu epic. I
lived easily with that darkness, that lack of knowledge. I never
thought to inquire further.

My mother's father had built a big house in Chaguanas.
I didn't know when. (It was in 1920; I was given that date in
1972.) He had gone back to India and died – in the life of our
family, a mythical event. (It occurred in 1926.) Little by little
I understood that this grandfather still had relations in India,
that there was a village, with an actual address. My mother,
giving me this address in 1961, recited it like poetry: district,
sub-district, village.

In 1962, at the end of a year of travel in India, I went to
that village. I wasn't prepared for the disturbance I felt,
turning off from the India where I had been a traveller, and
driving in a government jeep along a straight, dusty road to
another, very private world. Two ideas of history came
together during that short drive, two ways of thinking about
myself.

And there I discovered that to my grandfather this village

– the pond, the big trees he would have remembered, the brick dwellings with their enclosed courtyards (unlike the adobe and thatch of Trinidad Indian villages), the fields in the flat land, the immense sky, the white shrines – this village was the real place. Trinidad was the interlude, the illusion.

My grandfather had done well in Trinidad. He had bought much land – I continue to discover 'pieces' he had bought; he had bought properties in Port of Spain; he had established a very large family and in our community he had a name. But he was willing, while he was still an active man, to turn his back on this and return home, to the real place. He hadn't gone alone – a family secret suddenly revealed: he had taken another woman with him. But my grandfather hadn't seen his village again; he had died on the train from Calcutta. The woman with him had made her way to the village (no doubt reciting the address I had heard my mother recite). And there for all these years, in the house of my grandfather's brother, she had stayed.

She was very old when I saw her. Her skin had cracked; her eyes had filmed over; she moved about the courtyard on her haunches. She still had a few words of English. She had photographs of our family – things of Trinidad – to show; there remained to her the curious vanity that she knew us all very well.

She had had a great adventure. But her India had remained intact; her idea of the world had remained whole; no other idea of reality had broken through. It was different for thousands of others. In July and August 1932, during my father's first spell on the *Trinidad Guardian* (and around the time I was born), one of the big running stories in the paper was the repatriation of Indian immigrants on the *S.S. Ganges*.

Indian immigrants, at the end of their contract, were entitled to a small grant of land or to a free trip back to India with their families. The promise hadn't always been kept. Many Indians, after they had served out their indenture, had found themselves destitute and homeless. Such people, even within my memory, slept at night in the Port of Spain squares. Then in 1931 the *Ganges* had come, and taken away more than a thousand. Only 'paupers' were taken free; everyone else had to pay a small fare. The news, in 1932, that the *Ganges* was going to come again created frenzy in those who had been left behind the previous year. They saw this second coming of the *Ganges* as their last chance to go home, to be released from Trinidad. Many more wanted to go than could be taken on. A thousand left; a quarter were officially 'paupers'. Seven weeks later the *Ganges* reached Calcutta. And there, to the terror of the passengers, the *Ganges* was stormed by hundreds of derelicts, previously repatriated, who wanted now to be taken back to the other place. India for these people had been a dream of home, a dream of continuity after the illusion of Trinidad. All the India they had found was the area around the Calcutta docks.

Our own past was, like our idea of India, a dream. Of my mother's father, so important to our family, I grew up knowing very little. Of my father's family and my father's childhood I knew almost nothing. My father's father had died when my father was a baby. My father knew only his mother's stories of this man: a miserly and cruel man who counted every biscuit in the tin, made her walk five miles in the hot sun to save a penny fare, and, days before my father was born, drove her out of the house. My father never forgave his father. He forgave him only in a story he wrote, one of his stories of Indian village life, in which his mother's humiliation is made good by the ritual celebration of the birth of her son.

Another incident I knew about – and my father told this as a joke – was that at one time he had almost gone back to India on an immigrant ship. The family had been 'passed' for repatriation; they had gone to the immigration depot on Nelson Island. There my father had panicked, had decided that he didn't want to go back to India. He hid in one of the latrines overhanging the sea, and he stayed there until his mother changed her mind about the trip back to India.

This was what my father passed on to me about his family and his childhood. The events were as dateless as the home events of my own confused childhood. His early life seemed an extension back in time of my own; and I did not think to ask until much later for a more connected narrative. When I was at Oxford I pressed him in letters to write an autobiography. This was to encourage him as a writer, to point him to material he had never used. But some deep hurt or shame, something still raw and unresolved in his experience, kept my father from attempting any autobiographical writing. He wrote about other members of his family. He never wrote about himself.

It wasn't until 1972, when I was forty, and nearly twenty years after my father's death, that I got a connected idea of his ancestry and early life.

I was in Trinidad. In a Port of Spain shop one day the Indian boy who sold me a paper said he was related to me. I was interested, and asked him how – the succeeding generations, spreading through our small community, had added so many relations to those I had known. He said, quickly and precisely, that he was the grandson of my father's sister. The old lady was dying, he said. I should try to see her soon. I went the next morning.

Thirty years before, her house in the open country near Chaguanas had been one of the fairy-tale places my father had taken me to: the thatched hut with its swept yard, its mango tree, its hibiscus hedge, and with fields at the back. My father had written a story about her. But it was a long time before I understood that the story had been about her; that the story – again, a story of ritual and reconciliation – was about her unhappy first marriage; and that her life in that fairy-tale hut with her second husband, a man of a low, cultivator caste, was wretched.

That was now far in the past. Even the kind of countryside I associated with her had vanished, been built over. She was dying in a daughter's house on the traffic-choked Eastern Main Road that led out of Port of Spain, in a cool, airy room made neat both for her death and for visitors. She was attended by children and grandchildren, people of varying levels of education and skill; some had been to Canada. Here, as everywhere else in Trinidad, there had been movement: my father's sister, at the end of her life, could see success.

She was very small, and had always been very thin. Uncovered by blanket or sheet, in a long blue nightdress and a new, white, too-big cardigan, she lay very light, like an object carefully placed, on her spring mattress, over which the sheet had been pulled smooth and tight.

The cardigan, in the tropical morning, was odd. It was like a baby's garment, put on for her by someone else; like a tribute to her death, like the extravagant gift of a devoted daughter; and also like the old lady's last attempt at a joke. Like my father, whom she resembled, she had always been a humorist in a gathering (the gloom, the irritation, came immediately afterwards); and this death chamber was full of chatter and easy movement. There was even a camera; and she posed, willingly. One man, breezing in, sat down so hard on the bed that the old lady bumped up; and it seemed to be one of her jokes.

But her talk to me was serious. It was of caste and blood. When I was a child we hadn't been able to talk. I could follow Hindi but couldn't speak it. She couldn't speak a word of English, though nearly everyone around her was bilingual. She had since picked up a little English; and her death-bed talk, of caste and blood, was in this broken language. The language still strained her, but what she was saying was like her bequest to me. I had known her poor, living with a man of a cultivator caste. She wanted me to know now, before the knowledge vanished with her, what she – and my father – had come from. She wanted me to know that the blood was good.

She didn't talk of her second husband. She talked of the first. He had treated her badly, but what was important about him now was that he was a Punjabi brahmin, a 'scholar', she said, a man who could read and write Urdu and Persian. When she spoke of her father, she didn't remember the miserliness and cruelty which my father remembered. She wanted me to know that her father lived in a 'galvanize' house – a galvanized-iron roof being a sign of wealth, unlike thatch, which was what had sheltered her for most of her life.

Her father was a pundit, she said. And he was fussy; he didn't like having too much to do with the low. And here – since her face was too old to be moulded into any expression save one of great weariness – the old lady used her shrivelled little hand to make a gentle gesture of disdain. The disdain was for the low among Hindus. My father's sister had spent all her life in Trinidad; but in her caste vision no other community mattered or properly existed.

She took the story back to her father's mother. This was as far as her memory went. And for me it was far enough. With no dates, and no big external events to provide historical markers, I found it hard to hold this relationship in my head. But this story contained many of my father's sister's other stories; and it gave me something like a family history. In one detail it was shocking; but it all came to me as a fairy story. And I shall reconstruct it here as a story – momentarily keeping the characters at a distance.

About 1880, in the ancient town of Ayodhya in the United Provinces in India, a young girl of the Parray clan gave birth to a son. She must have been deeply disgraced, because she was willing to go alone with her baby to a far-off island to which other people of the region were going. That was how the Parray woman came to Trinidad. She intended her son to be a pundit; and in the district of Diego Martin she found a good pundit who was willing to take her son in and instruct him. (There was no hint, in the tale I heard, of sugar estates and barracks and contract labour.)

The years passed. The boy went out into the world and began to do pundit's work. He also dealt, in a small way, in the goods Hindus used in religious ceremonies. His mother began to look for a bride for him. Women of suitable caste and clan were not easy to find in Trinidad, but the Parray woman had some luck. It happened that three brothers of a suitable clan had made the journey out from India together, and it happened that one of these brothers had seven daughters.

The Parray boy married one of these daughters. They had three children, a girl and two boys. They lived in the village of Cunupia, not far from Chaguanas, in a house with adobe walls and a galvanized-iron roof. Quite suddenly, when the youngest child, a boy, was only two, the young Parray fell ill and died. Somehow all the gold coins he had hoarded disappeared; and the aunts and uncles thought the children and their mother should be sent back to India. Arrangements were made, but then at the last moment the youngest child didn't want to go. He ran away and hid in a latrine, and the ship sailed without them.

The family was scattered. The eldest child, a girl, worked in the house of a relative; she never learned to read or write. The elder boy went out to work on the sugar estates for eight cents a day. The younger boy was spared for school. He was sent to stay with his mother's sister, who had married a man who owned a shop and was starting a bus company. The boy went to school by day and worked until late at night in the shop.

The Parray woman lived on for some time, mourning her pundit son, whom she had brought from India as a baby. She always wore white for grief, and she became known in the country town of Chaguanas: a very small, even a dwarfish, woman with white hair and a pale complexion. She walked with a stick, and passed for a witch. Children mocked her; sometimes, as she approached, people drew the sign of the cross on the road.

The Parray woman was my father's grandmother. The Parray man who died young was my father's father. The elder boy who went out to work in the cane-fields became a small farmer; when he was old he would cry at the memory of those eight cents a day. The younger boy who was spared for school – in order that he might become a pundit and so fulfil the family destiny – was my father.

It is only in this story that I find some explanation of how, coming from that background, with little education and little English, in a small agricultural colony where writing was not an occupation, my father developed the ambition to be a writer. It was a version of the pundit's vocation. When I got to know my father – in Port of Spain, in 1938, when he was thirty-two and I was six – he was a journalist. I took his occupation for granted. It was years before I worked back to a proper wonder at his achievement.

5

The managing editor of the *Trinidad Guardian* from May 1929 to April 1934 was Gault MacGowan. I heard his name often when I was a child: he was the good man who had helped in the early days, and I was told that I had been shown to him as a baby one day in Chaguanas.

The Hindu who wants to be a pundit has first to find a guru. My father, wanting to learn to write, found MacGowan. It was MacGowan, my father said, who had taught him how to write; and all his life my father had for MacGowan the special devotion which the Hindu has for his guru. Even when I was at Oxford my father, in his letters to me, was passing on advice he had received twenty years before from

MacGowan. In 1951 he wrote: 'And as to a writer being hated or liked – I think it's the other way to what you think: a man is doing his work well when people begin *liking* him. I have never forgotten what Gault MacGowan told me years ago: "Write sympathetically"; and this, I suppose, in no way prevents us from writing truthfully, even brightly.'

MacGowan seems to have understood the relationship. In a letter he wrote me out of the blue in 1963, nearly thirty years after he had left Trinidad – a letter of pure affection, written to me as my father's son – MacGowan, then nearly seventy, living in Munich and 'still publishing', said he had always been interested in the people of India. He had found my father willing to learn, and had gone out of his way to instruct him.

An unlikely bond between the two men was a mischievous sense of humour. *Trinidad Hangman Disappointed – Robbed of Fee by Executive Council – Bitter Regret*. That was a MacGowan headline over a news item about a condemned man's reprieve. It was the kind of joke my father also relished. That particular headline was brought up in court, as an example of Mac-Gowan's irresponsibility, during one of the two big court cases MacGowan had in Trinidad. MacGowan said, 'Doesn't the headline tell the story? I think that just the word "robbed" is out of place.' Publicity like this wasn't unwelcome to MacGowan. He seems to have been litigious, and as a Fleet Street man he had the Fleet Street idea that a newspaper should every day in some way be its own news.

He had been brought out from England to Trinidad, on the recommendation of *The Times*, to modernize the *Trinidad Guardian*. The *Port of Spain Gazette*, founded in 1832, and representing French creole planter and business interests, was the established local paper. The *Guardian*, started in 1917, and representing other business interests, was floundering a long way behind. Its make-up was antiquated: on the front page a rectangle of closely printed news cables was set in a big frame of shop advertisements.

MacGowan changed the front page. He gave the *Guardian* a London look. He had a London feeling for international news (*Daily at Dawn – Last Night's News in London*). And to the affairs of multi-racial Trinidad he brought what, in local journalism, was absolutely new: a tourist's eye. Everything was worth looking at; there was a story in almost everything. And there were real excitements: French fugitives from Devil's Island, voodoo in negro backyards, Indian obeah, Venezuelan vampire bats (at one time the *Guardian* saw them flying about in daylight everywhere, and this concern with bats was to get both MacGowan and my father into trouble). Every community interested MacGowan. The Indians of the countryside were cut off by language, religion and culture from the rest of the colonial population. MacGowan became interested in them – as material, and also as potential readers.

It was as an Indian voice, a reforming, 'controversial' Indian voice (*Trinidad Indians Are Not Sincere*), that my father began to appear in MacGowan's *Guardian*, doing an occasional column signed 'The Pundit'. My feeling now is that these columns must have been rewritten by MacGowan, or (though my mother says no) that some of the material was plagiarized by my father from the reformist Hindu literature he had begun to read.

But a relationship was established between the two men. And my father – at a starting salary of four dollars a week – began to do reporting. There the voice was his own, the

knowledge of Trinidad Indian life was his own; and the zest
– for news, for the drama of everyday life, for human oddity
– the zest for looking with which MacGowan infected him
became real. He developed fast.

Even when there was no news, there could be news.
*Chaguanas Man Writes Lindbergh – 'I Know Where Your Baby Is'.
Indians Pray for Gandhi – Despair in Chaguanas.*

It must have been MacGowan who suggested to my father
that everybody had a story. Was that really so? Not far from
my mother's family house in Chaguanas was the railway crossing. Twice or four times a day an old one-armed negro closed
and opened the gates. Did that man have a story? The man
himself didn't seem to think so. He lived in absolute harmony
with the long vacancies of his calling, and the brightest thing
about my father's piece was MacGowan's headline: *Thirty-six
Years of Watching a Trinidad Railway Gate.*

More rewarding was the Indian shopkeeper a couple of
houses down on the other side of the road. He was a man of
the merchant caste who had come out to Trinidad as an indentured labourer. Field labour, and especially 'heading' manure,
carrying baskets of manure on his head, like untouchables in
India, had been a humiliation and a torment to him. In the
beginning he had cried at night; and sometimes his day's
'task' so wore him out that he couldn't cook his evening meal.
Once he had eaten a piece of sugar-cane in the field, and he
had been fined a dollar, almost a week's wage. But he had
served out his five-year indenture, and his caste instincts had
reasserted themselves. He had made money as a merchant
and was soon to build one of the earliest cinemas in the
countryside. It was a good story; in Trinidad at that time,
only my father could have done it.

MacGowan increased the circulation of the *Guardian*. But the directors of the paper had other local business interests as well, and they felt that MacGowan was damaging these interests. MacGowan, fresh from the depression in England, wanted to run a 'Buy British' campaign; the chairman of the *Guardian* directors owned a trading company which dealt in American goods. The chairman had land at Macqueripe Bay; MacGowan campaigned for a road to Maracas Bay, where the chairman had no land. Some of the directors had invested in tourist ventures; MacGowan was running stories in the *Guardian* about 'mad bats' that flew about in daylight, and his cables to *The Times* and *New York Times* about vampire bats and a special Trinidad form of rabies were said to be frightening away cruise ships.

Paralytic rabies was, in fact, killing cattle in Trinidad at this time. And for all the playfulness of his 'mad bat' campaign (*Join the Daylight Bat Hunt – Be First*), MacGowan was acting on good advice. A local French creole doctor had recently established the link between bats and paralytic rabies, and was experimenting with a vaccine; the work of this doctor, Pawan, was soon to be acknowledged in text-books of tropical medicine. But the *Guardian* chairman, who said later he had never heard of anyone in Trinidad dying from a bat bite, decided that MacGowan had to go.

MacGowan couldn't be sacked; he had his contract. He could, however, be attacked; and the editor of the *Port of Spain Gazette*, whom MacGowan had often satirized, was only too willing to help. *Scaremongering MacGowan Libels Trinidad in Two Continents*: this was a headline in the *Gazette* one day. MacGowan sued and won. Journalistically, the case was also a triumph: the *Guardian* and its editor had become serious news in both papers. It was even better journalism when MacGowan sued the *Guardian* chairman for slander. For three weeks, in a realization of a Fleet Street ideal, the *Guardian* became its own big news, with the chairman, the editor, and the editor's journalistic style getting full-page treatment day after day. But MacGowan lost the case. And all Trinidad knew what until then had been known only to a few: that at the end of his contract MacGowan would be leaving.

MacGowan left. My father stayed behind. He became disturbed, fell ill, lost his job, and was idle and dependent for four years. In 1938, in the house of my mother's mother in Port of Spain, he came fully into my life for the first time. And in his clippings book, an old estate wages ledger, I came upon his relics of his heroic and hopeful time with MacGowan.

This was, very roughly, what I knew when, two years after I had written about Bogart and the life of the street, I thought of reconstructing the life of someone like my father. I had changed flats in London; and my mind went back to 1938, to my discovery of the few pieces of furniture which my father had brought with him to Port of Spain, the first furniture I had thought of as mine. I wanted to tell the story of the life as the story of the acquiring of those simple, precious pieces. The book took three years to write. It changed; and the writing changed me. I was writing about things I didn't know; and the book that came out was very much my father's book. It was written out of his journalism and stories, out of his knowledge, knowledge he had got from the way of looking MacGowan had trained him in. It was written out of his writing.

The book was read some years later – in Moscow – by a *New York Times* writer, Israel Shenker. In 1970, in London, he interviewed me for his paper; he was doing a series on writers. Some weeks later he sent me a copy of a clipping from the *New York Herald Tribune* of 24 June 1933, and asked for my comments.

REPORTER SACRIFICES GOAT TO MOLLIFY HINDU GODDESS

Writer Kowtows to Kali to Escape Black Magic Death

Port of Spain, Trinidad, British West Indies.
June 23 (CP).

Threatened with death by the Hindu goddess Kali, Seepersad Naipaul, native writer, today offered a goat as sacrifice to appease the anger of the goddess.

Naipaul wrote newspaper articles revealing that native farmers of Hindu origin had defied government regulations for combating cattle diseases and had been substituting ancient rites of the goddess Kali to drive away the illness attacking their livestock.

The writer was told he would develop poisoning tomorrow, die on Sunday, and be buried on Monday unless he offered a goat sacrifice. Today he yielded to the entreaty of friends and relatives and made the demanded sacrifice.

I was staggered. I had no memory of this incident. I had read nothing about it in my father's ledger. I had heard nothing about it from my father or mother or anybody else. All that I remembered was that my father had a special horror of the Kali cult; and that he had told me once, with one of his rages about the family, that my mother's mother had been a devotee of Kali.

I wrote to Shenker that the story was probably one of MacGowan's joke stories, with my father trying to make himself his own news. That was what I believed, and the matter went to the back of my mind.

Two years later, when I was in Trinidad, I went to look at the *Guardian* file in the Port of Spain newspaper library. To me, until then, in spite of education, writing and travel, everything connected with my family past had seemed irrecoverable, existing only in fading memory. (All my father's documents, even his ledger, had been lost.)

Here were printed records. Here, in the sequence in which they had fallen in the mornings on the front steps of the Port of Spain house, were the *Guardian*s of 1938 and 1939, once looked at without being understood: the photographs of scholarship winners (such lucky men), the sports pages (with the same, often-used photographs of great cricketers), the cinema advertisements that had awakened such longing (Bobby Breen in *Rainbow on the River*).

And then, going back, I rediscovered parts of my father's ledger. I found that the ledger I had grown up with was not complete. My father had left out some things. The clipping Shenker had sent me told a true story. It was a bigger story than I had imagined, and it was not comic at all. It was the story of a great humiliation. It had occurred just when my father was winning through to a kind of independence, and had got started in his vocation. The independence was to go within months. The vocation – in a colonial Trinidad, without MacGowan – was to become meaningless; the vacancy was to be with my father for the rest of his life.

I had known about my father's long nervous illness. I hadn't known about its origins. My own ambitions had been seeded in something less than half knowledge of my father's early writing life.

6

My father, when I got to know him, was full of rages against my mother's family. But his early writings for the *Guardian* show that shortly after his marriage he was glamoured by the family.

They were a large brahmin family of landowners and pundits. Nearly all the sons-in-law were the sons of pundits, men with big names in our own private world, our island India. Caste had won my father admittance to the family, and for some time he seemed quite ready, in his *Guardian* reports, to act as a kind of family herald. *Popular Hindu Engagement – Chaguanas Link with Arouca*: MacGowan couldn't have known, but this item of 'Indian' news was really a family circular, court news: it was about the engagement of my grandmother's eldest granddaughter.

With the departure of my mother's father for India, and his subsequent death, the direction of the family had passed to the two eldest sons-in-law. They were brothers. They were ambitious and energetic men. They were concerned with the establishing of the local Hindu-Muslim school; with the affairs of the Local Road Board; and – in those days of the property franchise – with the higher politics connected with the island Legislative Council. They were also, as brahmins of the Tiwari clan, defenders of the orthodox Hindu faith – against Presbyterianism, then making converts among Hindus; and also against those reforming Hindu movements that had sent out missionaries from India. The brothers sought to be leaders; and they liked a fight. They were engaged in constant power games, which sometimes took a violent turn, with other families who also presumed to lead.

To belong to the family was to be in touch with much that was important in Indian life; or so my father made it. And in MacGowan's *Guardian* Indian news became mainly Chaguanas news, and Chaguanas news was often family news. *600 at Mass Meeting to Protest the Attitude of Cipriani.* That was news, but it was also a family occasion: the meeting had been convened by the two senior sons-in-law. And when three days later the Chaguanas correspondent reported that feeling against Cipriani (a local politician) was still so strong that an eleven-year-old boy had been moved to speak 'pathetically' at another public gathering, MacGowan couldn't have known that the boy in question was my mother's younger brother. (He became a Reader in mathematics at London University; and thirty years after his 'pathetic' speech he also became the first leader of the opposition in independent Trinidad.)

My father might begin a political item like this: 'At a surprise meeting last night . . .' And the chances were that the meeting had taken place in the 'hall', the big downstairs room in the wooden house at the back of the main family house in Chaguanas.

But this closeness to the news-makers of Chaguanas had its strains. The family was a totalitarian organization. Decisions

– about politics, about religious matters, and, most importantly, about other families – were taken by a closed circle at the top – my grandmother and her two eldest sons-in-law. Everyone in the family was expected to fall into line; and most people did. There was something like a family propaganda machine constantly at work. It strengthened approved attitudes; it could also turn inwards, to discredit and humiliate dissidents. There was no plan; it simply happened like that, from the nature of our family organization. (When the two senior sons-in-law were eventually expelled from the family, the machine was easily turned against them.) And even today, when I meet descendants of families who were once 'blacked' by my mother's family, I can feel I am in the presence of the enemy. To grow up in a family or clan like ours was to accept the ethos of the feud.

But what could be asked of a member of the family couldn't be asked of the reporter. The family had been strong supporters of the sitting member for the county in the Legislative Council. This man was a Hindu, and he was as good a legislator as the colonial constitution of the time permitted. Suddenly, perhaps for some Hindu sectarian reason, or because of a squabble over the running of the Hindu-Muslim school, our family decided to drop this man. They decided that at the next election, in 1933, they would support Mr Robinson, who was a white man and the owner of large sugar estates in the area.

Mr Robinson believed in child labour and his election speeches were invariably on this subject. He thought that any law that raised the school-leaving age to fourteen would be 'inhuman'. He was ready to be prosecuted 'a thousand times', he was ready to go to jail, rather than stop giving work to the children of the poor. One of our family's ruling sons-in-law made a similar speech. Mr Robinson, he said, was keeping young people out of jail.

It would not have been easy for my father, whose brother had gone to work as a child in the fields for eight cents a day, to be wholeheartedly on the family's side. But he tried; he gave a lot of attention to Mr Robinson. Then my father had to report that the two sons-in-law had been charged with uttering menaces (allegedly, a 'death threat') against someone on the other side.

Mr Robinson lost the election. This was more than political news. This was a family defeat which, because it was at the hands of another Hindu family, was like a family humiliation; and my father had to report it in the jaunty *Guardian* style. The day after the election there was a riot in Chaguanas. A Robinson crowd of about a thousand attacked a bus carrying exultant supporters of the other side. The bus drove through the attacking crowd; a man in the crowd was killed; a man in the bus had his arm torn off; the police issued seventy summonses. That also had to be reported. And it would not have been at all easy for my father to report that – after another violent incident – the two senior sons-in-law of the family had appeared in court and had been fined. The family house was on the main road. Only a few hundred yards away, in a cluster, were the official buildings: the railway station, the warden's office, the police station and the court-house. The reporter would have had no trouble getting his story and returning, as it were, to base.

So my father's position in the family changed. From being the reporter who could act as family herald, he became the reporter who got people into the paper whether they wanted it or not; he became a man on the other side.

And, in fact, in one important way my father had always been on the other side. The family, with all its pundits, were defenders of the orthodox Hindu faith. My father wasn't. Later – just ten years later – when we were living in Port of Spain and our Hindu world was breaking up, my father was to write lyrically about Hindu rituals and Indian village life. But when he was a young man this Indian life was all he knew; it seemed stagnant and enduring; and he was critical. He was not alone. He belonged, or was sympathetic, to the reforming movement known as the Arya Samaj, which sought to make of Hinduism a pure philosophical faith. The Arya Samaj was against caste, pundits, animistic ritual. They were against child marriage; they were for the education of girls. On both these issues they clashed with the orthodox. And even smaller issues, in Trinidad, could lead to family feuds. What was the correct form of Hindu greeting? Could marriage ceremonies take place in daylight? Or did they, as the orthodox insisted, have to take place at night?

It was as a reformer that my father had presented himself to MacGowan. And he had been encouraged by MacGowan: a 'controversial' reporter was better for the paper, and MacGowan's attitude to Indians was one of paternal concern. And it was as a reformer that my father tackled the Indian side of the paralytic rabies story.

There had been a recrudescence of the disease in the weeks following the election, and Hindus were still not having their cattle vaccinated. One reason was that the government charge was too high – twenty-four cents a shot, at a time when a labourer earned thirty cents a day. But there was also a strong religious objection. And in some villages, as a charm against the disease, there was a ceremony of sacrifice to Kali, the black mother-goddess. Women went in procession through five villages, singing, and asking for alms for Kali. With the money they got they bought a goat. On the appointed day the goat was garlanded, its head cut off, and its blood sprinkled on the altar before the image of the goddess.

This was the story my father wrote, a descriptive piece, naming no names. But the reformer could not stay his hand: he spoke of 'superstitious remedies' and 'amazing superstitious practices', and that was how MacGowan played it up. Ten days later – what deliberations took place in those ten days? – my father received an anonymous threatening letter in Hindi. The letter said he was to perform the very ceremony he had criticised, or he was going to die in a week.

There is an indication, from my father's reporting of the incident, that the threat came from within the ruling circle of the family, perhaps from one of the senior sons-in-law. This man, at any rate, when approached, offered no help and seemed anxious only to confirm the contents of the letter. And, in the abasement that was demanded of my father, there is something that suggests family cruelty: as though the reporter, the errant family member, was to be punished this time for all his previous misdemeanours and disloyalties.

In the week that followed my father existed on three planes. He was the reporter who had become his own very big front-page story: 'Next Sunday I am doomed to die.' He was the reformer who wasn't going to yield to 'ju-jus': 'I won't sacrifice a goat.' At the same time, as a man of feud-ridden Chaguanas, he was terrified of what he saw as a murder threat, and he was preparing to submit. Each role made nonsense of the other. And my father must have known it.

He wasn't going to sacrifice a goat to Kali. But then the readers of the *Guardian* discovered that he had made the sacrifice – not in Chaguanas, but in a little town a safe distance away.

A young English reporter, Sidney Rodin, who had been brought out recently by MacGowan to work on the *Guardian*, wrote the main story. It was a good piece of writing (and Rodin was to go back to London, to a long career in Fleet Street). Rodin's report, full of emotion, catches all the details that must have horrified my father: the goat anointed and garlanded with hibiscus; red powder on its neck to symbolize its own blood, its own life; the cutlass on the tree stump; the flowers and fruit on the sacrificial altar.

My father, in Rodin's account, is, it might be said, a little to one side: a man who (unknown to Rodin) had been intended by his grandmother and mother to be a pundit, now for the first time going through priestly rites: a man in white, garlanded like the goat with hibiscus, offering sacrificial clove-scented fire to the image of the goddess, to the still living goat, to the onlookers, and then offering the severed goat's head on a brass plate.

My father, in his own report accompanying Rodin's story, has very little to say. He has no means of recording what he felt. He goes back to the reformist literature he had read; he plagiarizes some paragraphs. And he blusters. He will never sacrifice again, he says; he knows his faith now. And he records it as a little triumph that he didn't wear a loincloth: he went through the ceremony in trousers and shirt. The odd, illogical bluster continues the next day, on the front page of the Sunday paper. *Mr Naipaul Greets You! – No Poison Last Night.* 'Good morning, everybody! As you behold, Kali has not got me yet . . .'

It was his last piece of jauntiness from Chaguanas. Two months later he worked on a big hurricane story, but that was in the south of the island. His reports from Chaguanas became intermittent, and then he faded away from the paper.

A few months later MacGowan left Trinidad. There was an idea that my father might go with MacGowan to the United States; and he took out a passport. But my father didn't go. Dread of the unknown overcame him, as it had overcome him when he was a child, waiting on Nelson Island for the ship to take him to India. The passport remained crisp and unused in his desk, with his incomplete ledger.

He must have become unbalanced. It was no help when the new editor of the *Guardian* took him off the staff and reduced him to a stringer. And soon he was quite ill.

I said to my mother one day when I came back from the Port of Spain newspaper library, 'Why didn't you tell me about the sacrifice?'

She said, simply, 'I didn't remember.' She added, 'Some things you will yourself to forget.'

'What form did my father's madness take?'

'He looked in the mirror one day and couldn't see himself. And he began to scream.'

The house where this terror befell him became unendurable to him. He left it. He became a wanderer, living in many different places, doing a variety of little jobs, dependent now on my mother's family, now on the family of his wealthy uncle by marriage. For thirteen years he had no house of his own.

My mother blamed MacGowan for the disaster. It gave her no pleasure to hear the name my father spoke so often or to follow MacGowan's later adventures. In 1942 we read in

Time magazine that MacGowan, then nearly fifty, had gone as a war correspondent on the Dieppe raid and had written his story immediately afterwards, keeping himself awake (a MacGowan touch) on Benzedrine. And the *Guardian*, relenting towards its former editor, reported in 1944 that Mac-Gowan had been taken prisoner by the Germans in France but had managed to escape, jumping off a train.

I understand my mother's attitude, but it isn't mine. It was no fault of MacGowan's that he had the bigger world to return to, and my father had only Trinidad. MacGowan transmitted his own idea of the journalist's or writer's vocation to my father. From no other source in colonial Trinidad could my father have got that. No other editor of the *Guardian* gave my father any sense of the worth of his calling. It was the idea of the vocation that exalted my father in the Mac-Gowan days. It was in the day's story, and its reception by a sympathetic editor, that the day's struggle and the day's triumph lay. He wrote about Chaguanas, but the daily exercise of an admired craft would, in his own mind, have raised him above the constrictions of Chaguanas: he would have grown to feel protected by the word, and the quality of his calling. Then the props went. And he had only Chaguanas and Trinidad.

Admiration of the craft stayed with him. In 1936, in the middle of his illness – when I would have been staying in Chaguanas at my mother's family house – he sent me a little book, *The School of Poetry*, an anthology, really a decorated keepsake, edited by Alice Meynell. It had been marked down by the shop from forty-eight cents to twenty-four cents. It was his gift to his son of something noble, something connected with the word. Somehow the book survived all our moves. It is inscribed: 'To Vidyadhar, from his father. Today you have reached the span of 3 years, 10 months and 15 days. And I make this present to you with this counsel in addition. Live up to the estate of man, follow truth, be kind and gentle and trust God.'

Two years later, when my father got his *Guardian* job back, we moved to the house in Port of Spain. It was for me the serenest time of my childhood. I didn't know then how close my father was to his mental illness; and I didn't understand how much that job with the *Guardian* was for him a daily humiliation. He had had to plead for the job. In the desk were the many brusque replies, which I handled lovingly and often for the sake of the raised letter-heads.

Among the books in the bookcase were the books of comfort my father had picked up during his lost years: not only Marcus Aurelius and Epictetus, but also many mystical or quasi-religious books. One healing incantation from the time of his illness I got to know, because he taught it to me. It was a line he had adapted from Ella Wheeler Wilcox: 'Even this shall pass away.' It was an elastic consolation. It could deal with the pain of a moment, a day, life itself.

He never talked about the nature of his illness. And what is astonishing to me is that, with the vocation, he so accurately transmitted to me – without saying anything about it – his hysteria from the time when I didn't know him: his fear of extinction. That was his subsidiary gift to me. That fear became mine as well. It was linked with the idea of the vocation: the fear could be combated only by the exercise of the vocation.

And it was that fear, a panic about failing to be what I should be, rather than simple ambition, that was with me when I came down from Oxford in 1954 and began trying to write in London. My father had died the previous year. Our family was in distress. I should have done something for them, gone back to them. But, without having become a writer, I couldn't go back. In my eleventh month in London I wrote about Bogart. I wrote my book; I wrote another. I began to go back.

July–October 1982

THE CROCODILES OF YAMOUSSOUKRO

I

Yamoussoukro, a place deep in the wet forests of the Ivory Coast, is one of the wonders of black Africa. It used to be a village, and perhaps then it was like some other West African bush villages, where grass huts perish after two years. But Yamoussoukro was also the seat of a regional tribal chief; and during the half a century or so of direct French rule in the interior, the authority of the chieftaincy – moral, or spiritual, or magical authority – was not forgotten.

The very old man who is still chief received a French education. He became what the French called a 'colonial' doctor – not the finished French product, but a doctor nonetheless. Later he became a politician, a protest leader. With independence in 1960 – the bush returned with alterations to its people – he began to rule the Ivory Coast. And he has ruled ever since.

He has ruled well. He has used the French as technicians, advisers, administrators; and, with no ready-made mineral wealth, with the resources only of tropical forests and fields, he has made his country rich. So rich, that the Ivory Coast imports labour from its more depressed or chaotic African neighbours. Labour immigration, as much as natural increase, has raised the population from three million in 1960 to nine million today. Abidjan, the capital, begun unpromisingly on the black mud of a fetid lagoon, has become one of the biggest ports in West Africa. And one hundred and fifty miles inland, at the end of an auto-route that would not disgrace France itself, the president's ancestral village of Yamoussoukro has been transformed.

The ancestral village has in fact vanished from public sight. The entire village – huts (if they still survive), common ground, the semi-sacred palaver tree – has been incorporated into the grounds of a new presidential palace. And all is hidden by a high palace wall that must be many miles long.

Down one side of the palace there is an artificial lake, and in this lake turtles and man-eating crocodiles have been introduced. These are totemic, emblematic creatures, and they belong to the president. There were no crocodiles in Yamoussoukro before. No one knows precisely what they mean. But to all Africans they speak at once of danger and of the president's, the chief's, magically granted knowledge of his power as something more than human, something emanating from the earth itself.

The power and wisdom of the chief have caused the forest around Yamoussoukro to disappear. Where once were African fields, unused common land, and wild trees there are now ordered, mechanized plantations. For square mile upon square mile mangoes, avocadoes or pineapples grow in straight lines, the straight lines that are beautiful to people to whom Nature is usually formless, unfriendly bush. Land in this part of Africa, it is said, belongs to the user; there can be no title in bush. And until they were given to the state some years ago, these plantations around Yamoussoukro were the president's personal estates.

The president's ideas have always been big, and his plans for Yamoussoukro are very big. He would like it to be one of the great cities of Africa and the world. The land has been levelled, and avenues as wide as runways outline the metropolis that is to be. Extravagant and sometimes brilliant modern buildings have been set down in the stripped wilderness and await full use.

To attract visitors, there is a great golf course, beautifully landscaped and so far steadfastly maintained against the fast-growing bush. It is the president's idea, though he doesn't play golf himself. The golf idea came to him when he was old, and now in his benign, guiding way he would like all his people, all the sixty or so tribes of the Ivory Coast, to take up golf. To house the visitors, there is a twelve-storey Hotel President, one of the French Sofitel hotel chain. The hotel brochure is printed in France; its silvery grey cover looks princely. 'Find the traces of the native village of President Houphouët-Boigny,' the brochure says, 'and discover the ultra-modern prefiguration of the Africa of tomorrow.'

The two ideas go together. The ultra-modern dream also serves old Africa. It is pharaonic: it has a touch of the antique world. Away from the stupendous modern frivolities of the golf course and the golf club and the swimming pool of the Hotel President there is the presidential palace with its artificial lake. Outside the blank walls that hide the president's ancestral village and the palaver tree from the common view, the president's totemic crocodiles are fed with fresh meat every day. People can go and watch. But distances in Yamoussoukro are so great, and the scarred, empty spaces so forbidding, that only people with cars can easily go; and they tend to be visitors, tourists.

The feeding ritual takes place in the afternoon, in bright light. There are the cars, the tourists in bright clothes, the cameras. But the crocodiles are sacred. A live offering – a chicken – has to be made to them; it is part of the ritual. This element of sacrifice, this protracted display of power and cruelty, is as unsettling as it is meant to be, and it seems to bring night and the forest close again to the dream of Yamoussoukro.

To the man from outside, whatever his political or religious faith, Africa can often seem to be in a state of becoming. It is always on the point of being made something else. So it arouses hope, ambition, frustration, irritation. And even the success of the Ivory Coast induces a kind of anxiety. Will it last? Will the Africans be able to take over from the French and the Israelis and the others who have built it all for them and still effectively run it?

And then at a place like Yamoussoukro, where the anxiety becomes most acute, it also begins to feel unreal. You get a glimpse of an African Africa, an Africa which – whatever the accidents of history, whatever the current manifestations of earthly glory – has always been in its own eyes complete, achieved, bursting with its own powers.

This idea of African completeness should not have surprised me. Something like this, a similar religious feeling, was, fleetingly, at the back of many of the slave revolts in the Caribbean. The idea of African completeness endures in various Caribbean religious cults; and touches the politics of the region. Many of the recent political movements in the black Caribbean have had a millenarian, ecstatic, purely African side.

West Africa peopled the slave plantations of the New World. But that wasn't the idea I took to the Ivory Coast. I went for simpler reasons. The world is too various; it can exist only in compartments in our minds. I wanted to be in

West Africa, where I had never been; I wanted to be in a former French territory in Africa; and I wanted to be in an African country which, in the mess of black Africa, was generally held to be a political and economic success. African success, France in Africa – those were the glamorous ideas that took me out.

France in Africa was a private fantasy. It was based on my own love of the French language, a special schoolboy love, given me at Queen's Royal College in colonial Trinidad by teachers, many of them black or partly black, who were themselves in love with the French language and an idea (hinted at, never stated) of an accepting, assimilating France. France in Africa: I imagined the language in the mouths of elegant Africans; I thought of tall, turbanned women, like those of Mali and the Congo; I thought of wine and tropical boulevards.

But in the humidity of the Ivory Coast, the wine (stupefying at lunchtime) was mainly rosé and Moroccan; West African French was as broken and sourly accented as West African English; and there was nothing like a boulevard in the hard little commercial centre of Abidjan, where, here and there in the shadows of tall new buildings, Lebanese shops still spoke of a recent, duller colonial township. Instead of boulevards there was the African hubbub of 'popular' African areas. Away from that there was – as in many other former colonial territories – the ready-made, enclosed glamour of new international hotels.

Around the swimming pool of the Forum Golf Hotel the small-breasted wives of French businessmen and technicians sunbathed topless, among the black-and-orange lizards. Africa came on at night, as the cabaret: not the Africa of the night clubs in the African areas, but the Africa of officially approved 'culture': the semi-religious or magical dances of the forest, done now in a landscaped garden, electric light playing on the big, bare breasts of dancing, chanting women.

I hadn't really thought I would find France in Africa – it was a fantasy. But I hadn't expected that in the Ivory Coast France and Africa would still be like separate ideas. It made more puzzling the success that was to be seen in the great capital city of Abidjan: in the urban highways, with direction boards that suggested France; the skyscrapers of the city centre; the university campus and the golf course; the spreading workers' areas, disordered but not poor; the many mixed – African and European – middle-class residential areas; the blocks of government-built flats; the big port and industrial zone; the tainted tropical lagoon reflecting at dusk the lights of the rush-hour traffic on the 'corniche'.

'Isn't it wonderful,' an American from the embassy said to me one evening, looking at that view, 'that they have done this with just a little bit of coffee and a little bit of cocoa?'

Out of apparently little, wealth had been created. And this wealth had been shared and used. The Ivory Coast boom had now abated. Coffee prices had dropped by a third and cocoa by a half, and the oil exploration people were leaving the Ivory Coast for other French African countries. There was some discontent now; protests had begun to be heard about the number of French people in the country. But something extraordinary had been achieved; in this corner of Africa even the continuing order of the state was like a miracle.

All around was chaos or nullity. Liberia, illiterate, impoverished, was ruled by its army after members of the previous government had been unceremoniously shot on the beach. (What pictures those news reports gave to the mind: the holiday setting, the bewildered men in suits or pyjamas, the uniformed men with guns, the sound of the sea.) Guinea, once like the Ivory Coast a French colony, and potentially richer than the Ivory Coast, was now bankrupt, a murderous tyranny, famous for the 'black diet' of its condemned cells, where people were given neither food nor water and simply left to waste away. Ghana, at the time of its independence in 1957 far richer and better educated than the Ivory Coast, with institutions, was now after repeated coups in a state of anarchy, a source of migrant labour.

Yet, tribally speaking, the people of Ghana and Guinea were like some of the people of the Ivory Coast. The tribes, the *ethnies*, were not contained within national borders. And though the Ivory Coast was said to be liberal, it was also an African state, a one-party state, with its own cult of the leader: the man who had become president at independence had never stopped being president. What had been done in the Ivory Coast hadn't been done suddenly; it had been sustained over more than twenty years. Clearly, then, to explain this African success, there had been – over and above the personality of the president – some principle of organization that suited the people, something easily grasped and repeatable.

The explanations given to the visitor were simple, short, polished: they had been given to many other visitors before. The nationalist movement in a country like Ghana had been a movement of clerks and lawyers, ideologues seeking at once to ennoble and Africanize Africa by foreign ideas. The nationalist movement in the Ivory Coast had been simpler, a movement of farmers, *planteurs*, village people.

This was added to by an ambassador I saw not long after I arrived. The news he had just received was of the putting down of yet another coup in Ghana. The two countries were different at independence, the ambassador said. They shared only the climate and the vegetation. In Ghana after independence the nationalists concentrated on 'administrative structures'. In the Ivory Coast they concentrated on creating wealth, wealth from peasant farming. They were less concerned with Africanization. They built roads, to bring the villages closer to the market place. They gave the villages services and security – and security was important. They tried to keep people on the land by ending the isolation of the villages; and they had succeeded. There were now roads and hotels all over the Ivory Coast. The president's village of Yamoussoukro in the centre of the country was now just a three-hour drive from Abidjan.

That was how I first heard of Yamoussoukro. It was the president's village, and it might have been no more than one of the farming villages opened up by a government concerned with agriculture.

Ambassadors have to choose their words. They do a specialized job and it is necessary for them to live ceremonial lives. As officials, their vision of a country shouldn't run too far beyond that of the local people with whom they have to deal. So, with ambassadors as with other expatriates in black Africa, there appears at a first meeting a kind of ambivalence. To say what they feel they have to say they appear to be denying or ignoring part of what they know. Expatriates may know African Africa, but this is not the Africa they put forward to a visitor at a first meeting. They are men with jobs, skills; their job is part of their self-esteem; and the Africa they present to the visitor is the Africa connected with their jobs. The ambivalence is natural; it is not disingenuous. The doing of certain kinds of work in Africa, the practice of certain disciplines or skills from another civilization, can be like a disinterested exercise of virtue. Many expatriates – those who last in freed black Africa – become genuinely good people; and not a few are oddly solitary.

It was from Philip, an expatriate, that I next heard of Yamoussoukro. Philip was English. He was in his late thirties, and much of his working life had been spent in Africa. He now worked for an inter-state African organization. His wife was a black Guyanese girl of great beauty, from a family settled in England. It was odd, Philip said, that he should be the African side of their marriage, and Janet the English, 'from Huddersfield'.

Her birthday fell that weekend. And, to celebrate, they were going on the expatriate Sunday excursion to Grand-Bassam on the beach. I went with their party: out of Abidjan, past the shack settlements of migrant labourers, past the coconut estates with coconut trees planted in rows and offering long vistas down the cleared spaces between the trees, past the lines of thatched huts selling African curios and artefacts, to the ruined old colonial capital of Grand-Bassam, abandoned after a yellow fever epidemic in 1899, concrete and corrugated iron and streets of thick dust, and at last the thatched Sunday restaurants on the sea: the excursion that, as I was to discover at the end of my second week, was part of the routine and tedium and constriction of expatriate life.

On the edge of Abidjan the highway became very wide,

without any median divider. It was like that, Philip said, for parades.

'It's like Yamoussoukro,' Philip said. 'You should try to get there. Try to get there at night. You'll see the double row of lights. You'll wonder where you are. And in the morning you'll see that you are nowhere.'

We passed low army barracks. They seemed to go on for a long time. They were the barracks of a French Foreign Legion regiment. They kept a low profile, Philip said. They were in the Ivory Coast only to train.

I said to him, 'Does it depress you, being in all these African countries with their separate personality cults?'

It was too strong a question to put to him at this stage of our relationship.

He said, 'There is the cult of personality everywhere. Looking at the Falklands business from the outside, I would say there was a great cult of the personality there. Mrs Thatcher raised herself up.'

I asked whether he really thought that the situations were the same.

He said with unexpected directness, 'No.' And a little while later he returned to the subject, as though to explain both himself and what he had said. 'You must understand that Africans like the cult of personality better. It is what they understand. A multiplicity of parties and personalities confuses them. I've seen this happen.'

And African attitudes to authority was one of the subjects that came up at an embassy lunch the next day. The president, I heard, had become aware of the growing discontent in the Ivory Coast. In his benignity, and out of his wish to do the right thing, he had tried to 'democratize'. There was only one party in the Ivory Coast, and normally at elections there was only one list of candidates; people in any particular constituency simply voted for or against the party's candidate. At the last election there had been an experiment. It was decreed that anyone in the party could contest any seat. For the 140 or so seats in the assembly there had been more than 600 candidates; and eighty per cent of the old deputies, some of whom had held their seats for twenty years, had been voted out.

Democracy of a kind had been served, but there had been a more than political consternation. The old deputies had built up followings; they had become elders; and in the African tradition an elder remained an elder till he died. A man stripped of authority couldn't simply go back to being an ordinary villager; he had been personally degraded. So the democratic experiment had damaged the cohesiveness of village life. Ever since the election there had been any number of programmes on the television about the need for 'reconciliation'. 'Democracy', people's rule, was the imported idea; reconciliation was the African idea – in certain villages, among certain tribes, there actually was an annual ceremony of reconciliation, presided over by the local chief.

And – though the link wasn't made at the lunch – just as it was hard for an elder or deputy to stop being what he was, so it was hard for the president to stop being president, though he was now very old, eighty or more – no one really knew his age. An added reason for the president's holding on was the great enterprise of Yamoussoukro. The work there was far from completed, would not be completed in the president's lifetime. And that was why, democrat and anti-tribalist though he was, the president would have to choose as his successor someone from his own dominant Baoulé tribe. That was the only way he had of ensuring, or trying to ensure, that the work on Yamoussoukro would go on after his death.

So, as I heard about it, Yamoussoukro grew: from being an agricultural village in the interior, provided now with roads and services; to a place with very wide, brilliantly lit avenues that led nowhere; to a monumental city meant to make an African ruler immortal. And even as I understood the pharaonic scale of the project, I feared for it. I thought of the monuments of ancient Egypt where the cartouches of one pharaoh could be defaced by his successors; where the carved and polished stones of the monument of one sacred pharaoh could be broken up and used unceremoniously, as building blocks alone, in the monument of another. And this African dream of Yamoussoukro was being created by people of another civilization: French and Israelis and others, whose skills might easily vanish from the continent.

So the first impressions of modern African success began to be qualified. Success became an expression of the non-ideological personality of the ruler, the man of an established ruling family; this rested on an African idea of authority. And at the bottom of it all was magic.

This last idea, of magic, didn't come to me by any secret means. I came upon it openly, in the newspapers.

There was one daily newspaper in the Ivory Coast; at least, only one came my way. It was called *Fraternité Matin*. Every day on its front page, in the top left-hand corner, it carried a 'thought' of the president's. The thoughts were mainly about development and the economy; and so were the big front-page stories. There were sports pages. But they didn't make the paper any less austere. There was no gossip, almost nothing from the police. *Fraternité Matin* suggested a nation at work and at school – even night school. But then, at the end of my first week, there was something like a real news story. It was spread over two inside pages of the weekend issue and was clearly about a well-known local sensation.

Seventeen kilometres out of Abidjan, in a village on the great auto-route to Yamoussoukro, there was a school-teacher's house which from time to time blazed with mysterious fires. A reader had written to the paper that weekend with the suggestion that there was probably some escape of natural gas in the neighbourhood. But this letter, headed 'A Scientific Solution', was placed at the bottom of the right-hand page. The main story, the *reportage*, was that the mystery of the fires at Kilometre 17 had been solved.

It had been solved by a preacher of the Celestial Christian sect. Even before they had been called in on the case – and while the teacher was spending a fortune on fetish-makers and Muslim magicians – the Celestial Christians had 'discovered' through some divine communication that the Evil Spirit was at the bottom of the business. In investigations of this kind, according to the Celestial Christians, there were two levels that had to be considered, the mystical and the human. At the mystical level there was the Evil Spirit. At the human level, there was the person who had been possessed by the Evil Spirit and turned into a fire-raiser.

The Celestial Christians, with their special gifts, had found out who this person was. And the Evil Spirit, discovered in this way, was immediately at a disadvantage. The Spirit had gone to the Celestial Christians and pleaded with them to be left in peace, to get on with its wicked work in the Ivory Coast in secret. It had offered bribes. The Celestial Christians refused. However, they engaged the Evil Spirit in dialogue. They asked the Evil Spirit why it wanted to start fires in the schoolteacher's house. The Spirit didn't answer directly. It only said, 'in a mystical way', that it was the owner of the house. This was apparently a frightening reply, and the Celestial Christians didn't wait to hear any more. They at once ordered the Evil Spirit not only to leave the house but also to get out of the Ivory Coast altogether. And the Spirit meekly went.

Now a protective cross was planted outside the schoolteacher's front door, and peace had returned to the tormented man. The Celestial Christians, making the most of their success, regretted only that the schoolteacher had spent so much money on fetishes and Muslim *marabout* magic. They, the Christians, had done what they had done only with their faith in Jesus Christ and a few candles.

So the story of Kilometre 17 had had a happy ending. It was a moral story; and like so much else in *Fraternité Matin*, it seemed to have an element of benign instruction and reassurance. The Evil Spirit had been defeated by a stronger force. More than the peace of mind of a village schoolteacher had been secured: the Ivory Coast itself had been cleansed.

The report in *Fraternité Matin* didn't say who the possessed person was. This might have been due to legal caution or more probably to some taboo about the Evil Spirit. The reporter only dropped hints: the possessed person was in and out of the house, was well known to the schoolteacher's family, did many things for the schoolteacher. The Sunday magazine, *Ivoire Dimanche*, in a two-page photographic feature on the case, showed photographs of the teacher and his two wives. Was the possessed person one of the wives? Both women looked equally enervated, as enervated as the teacher himself, though they were thin and he was plump. The presence of sorcery and the Evil Spirit seemed to have given them all a glimpse of hell. Sorcery was no joke; and the cover story of *Ivoire Dimanche* was, in fact, about the war of true religion and good magic against sorcery and bad magic.

The visitor saw the highways and skyscrapers of Abidjan, and he thought of development and African success. But Abidjan was in Africa, and in the minds of the people the world was to be made safe in another way as well. The reassuring message in the government-controlled press was that there was light at either end of the African tunnel.

2

I travel to discover other states of mind. And if for this intellectual adventure I go to places where people live restricted lives, it is because my curiosity is still dictated in part by my colonial Trinidad background. I go to places which, however alien, connect in some way with what I already know. When my curiosity has been satisfied, when there are no more surprises, the intellectual adventure is over and I become anxious to leave.

It is a writer's curiosity rather than an ethnographer's or journalist's. So while, when I travel, I can move only according to what I find, I also live, as it were, in a novel of my own making, moving from not knowing to knowing, with person interweaving with person and incident opening out into incident. The intellectual adventure is also a human one: I can move only according to my sympathy. I don't force anything; there is no spokesman I have to see, no one I absolutely must interview. The kind of understanding I am looking for comes best through people I get to like. And in the Ivory Coast I moved in the main among expatriates, white and black. I saw the country through them and through their varied experience.

One of these expatriates was Terry Shroeder, the public affairs officer of the American embassy. He was in his late forties, and a bachelor, a slender, handsome man with the kind of melancholy that attracts and resists women. He was going to retire early from the foreign service. The Ivory Coast was his last posting but one, and he was at the very end of his time there. It was Terry who had given me the phrase about 'a little bit of coffee and a little bit of cocoa'. He admired the economic achievements of the Ivory Coast. But he also had a feeling for its African side.

It was Terry who at our first meeting told me that there was in the Ivory Coast a famous and very old African sage who was the president's spiritual counsellor. The sage was open to other consultation as well, and Terry would have liked me to see him. But the sage was unfortunately 'hospitalized', and remained so during my time in the Ivory Coast. The name of the sage was Amadou Hampaté Bâ. He had been in his time an ambassador, and a member of an important Unesco body; but his fame in the Ivory Coast was spiritual, and rested on his mastery of arithmology and other esoteric studies. Terry knew him well enough to visit him in hospital, and he always referred to him as Mr Hampaté Bâ ('Hampaté' not far off in sound from 'Humpty'). Hampaté Bâ was a Muslim from Mali, to the north; but he had a large place in his heart for African religion. 'Islam is my father, but Africa is my mother' – this, according to Terry, was one of Hampaté Bâ's well-known sayings. Another saying was: 'Whenever an old man dies in Africa, a library has burned down.'

At our first meeting Terry also told me about someone who was doing research among the village witch-doctors or medicine men. Some of these men did possess knowledge of a sort. They could deal in an African way with African neuroses; they also knew about herbs and poisons. They were secretive about the poisons. Their knowledge of poisons made them feared and was one of the sources of their power.

This talk of poison made me think of the Caribbean islands on the other side of the ocean. In the old days, on the slave plantations there, constantly replendished with 'new negroes' (as they were called) from places like the Ivory Coast, poison had been one of the special terrors of slaves and slave-owners. Some poisoner was always about; in the slave underground or underworld, the hidden Africa of the plantations, someone could usually be found with a stock of poison; and a vengeful slave could do terrible things. In Trinidad in 1794 a hundred negroes were poisoned on the Coblenz estate in Port of Spain, and the estate had to be abandoned. In 1801, when the estate was bought by the emigré Baron de Montalembert, a poisoner went to work again, and in the first month of his proprietorship the baron lost 120 of the 140 'seasoned' negroes he had put in.

As much as poison, the plantation owners in the Caribbean feared African magic. Slavery depended on obedience, on the acceptance by the slave of the logic of his position. A persuasive magician, awakening African instincts, could give his fellows a sense of the unreality of the workaday world, and could incite normally docile and even loyal slaves to rebellion. Magicians, once they were identified, were treated with great severity. In Trinidad and Martinique they could be burned alive.

Magic and poison – in the old documents of the islands, they had seemed like the weapons of despair; and they probably had been. Here in the Ivory Coast they were part of a world that was still whole. The African culture that was officially promoted, and could at times seem to be only a source of tourist motifs, was an expression of African religion. Even in the masks in the souvenir shops, even in the dances beside the swimming pool of the Forum Golf Hotel, there was a feeling of awe, a radiation of accepted magical practices. Men here knew another reality; they lived easily in a world of spirit and spirits.

And it was Terry Shroeder who introduced me to Arlette. Arlette was a black woman from Martinique. Her French, beautifully enunciated, revived all my schoolboy love of the language. She was in her late thirties or early forties, a big woman, full of friendship, generous with her time and knowledge; she was to make me understand many things about the country. She had married an Ivorian, whom she had met in Paris, and she had lived for twenty years in the Ivory Coast. She was divorced now; her former husband had gone to Gabon, the newest French African land of oil and money. Arlette worked in an arts department of the university in Abidjan. She lived by herself; she had many friends in the foreign community; I felt she feared solitude. She was an expatriate – expatriates in the Ivory Coast were black as well as white.

Martinique, France, French-speaking Africa: the chain was obvious, and at one time – when I was at school in cramped Trinidad, learning French from black men who had a high idea of a welcoming, liberating French culture – Arlette's life journey would have seemed to me romantic. But when I had thought of going to the Ivory Coast, I hadn't thought of French West Indians making the roundabout journey back. So, in addition to the connections I could make for myself, other connections were offered to me. And the Ivory Coast became different from the country I had imagined.

We met Arlette at a piano recital sponsored by the Goethe Institute, the cultural wing of the West German embassy. Terry was going partly to give support to a fellow diplomat: these cultural evenings arranged by foreign embassies could be poorly attended. The Ivorians – rich, successful, served by foreign labour – were blasé about foreigners in general; it wasn't easy to entice them, Terry said. At his own cultural evenings Terry offered dinner beforehand, and hoped that people would stay on. It didn't always work. Foreign culture was too foreign. The biggest American event in the Ivory Coast had been the recent visit of the U.S.S. *Portland*, when the Americans, using marvellous landing craft, had staged a demonstration assault on an island off the coast.

Terry said, with melancholy pride, 'That impressed the Ivorian military.'

Arlette lived in a government flat, in a compound full of blocks of government flats. We couldn't find her when we went to pick her up. We went on to the Goethe Institute. She was there, waiting in the garden, a big, dark-brown woman in a shiny white dress, looking a little forlorn in the lamplight and tree shadows. She was chewing; she was always nervously chewing, or sucking on a sweet, or eating something. They had cut off the water to her flat, she said. She had objected to the bill, refused to pay; and they had cut the water off. Now she was using the bathrooms of various friends. (She fought that water battle for some days; but then she paid the bill.)

The audience for the piano recital was white. The pianist that the Goethe Institute was offering to French-speaking Africa was an Alsatian with a French name. He had done the French African circuit before for the Institute, and had a local reputation. He was a tall, thin, half-smiling man in chunky black shoes, and with strong, big, white hands. When applause came, he bowed, picked his way down two shaky, detachable steps from the platform, walked briskly to the end of the hall as though he was leaving us forever, but then he waited in the shadows, walked back to the platform, up the shaky steps, and bowed again. At the end he walked back twice and played two encores.

Arlette said in French, 'I had a bet with Terry that there would be only ten black faces here. I was wrong. There are only three.' Africans didn't like cultural music, Arlette said. They liked only African night-club music. Even in Paris that was what African students looked for. But still, Arlette said, shaking her head to the rhythm of her French speech, and acknowledging her own restlessness during the recital, the pianist had chosen some difficult pieces, *des morceaux difficiles*.

The pianist and the German cultural counsellor stood at the door to say goodbye. The pianist was neat and silent, black-suited. The counsellor was artistically casual, with big round glasses and a full round head of long red hair. He was pleased with the success of his evening. It was expensive, he said to Terry, putting on music of that quality. The Goethe Institute in Abidjan could do this kind of thing only once a year. The pianist should have been going on to Accra in Ghana, but – and the counsellor gave a diplomatic shrug, as though we all knew about events in Ghana, and it wasn't for him to comment.

We went afterwards, Arlette and I, to Terry's house. It was a bachelor's house. The sitting room was large and formal; many of Terry's cultural evenings took place there. There were mementoes of the East, where Terry had served, and there were African masks and objects. Terry offered wine, and went to the kitchen to make scrambled eggs.

Arlette told me about the French. She loved the culture of France, she said. But she detested the manners, *les moeurs*. She meant that the French were socially rigid and petty, extraordinarily fussy about having the correct glasses, the correct cutlery, the right wines. For the *petits français* – and especially in a place like Abidjan – these things were like moral issues. And there was the French obsession with food. It was part of the French myth, but Arlette didn't admire it. How could you admire people who, when you got back from a foreign country, could only think of asking: '*Mange-t-on bien là?*' 'Is the food good there?'

Arlette said that in the Ivory Coast the French West Indians, *les antillais*, behaved like French people. They looked down on the Africans and – because they thought of themselves as civilized and French – they expected the Africans to look up to them. '*Mais ils sont déçus.*' The West Indians made an error; Africans looked up to nobody; and life was as a result full of stress for some West Indians in the Ivory Coast.

So, in spite of what she had said about Africans and night-club music, Arlette separated herself both from French people and from a certain kind of French West Indian. And it was also clear that, in spite of her failed African marriage and her present solitude, there was in her some deep feeling for the Africa that followed its own ways.

At our supper of eggs and brown bread and wine, the talk turned to Amadou Hampaté Bâ, the sage who was the president's spiritual counsellor.

Arlette said, with glittering eyes, 'He's a great man. One of the great men of Africa.'

Terry had a spare copy of Hampaté Bâ's booklet, *Jésus Vu par un Musulman*, 'Christ Seen by a Muslim'. The book had been presented nineteen months before by the sage to Flora Lewis of the *New York Times* and inscribed to her in a shaky hand.

It was in this copy that, later that night, I read of the arithmological calculations which, applied to invocations and other religious formulae, proved the essential oneness of Islam and Christianity.

Hampaté Bâ described himself as 'a man of dialogue', and the last chapter of his little book was about the president of the Ivory Coast. He said that he and the president often had long spiritual discussions when the president's state duties permitted. He had asked the president one day for some story, some legend acquired perhaps from an African elder, that might serve as a parable of brotherly love. And the president had told Hampaté Bâ this story.

'There was a captive at the royal court of Yamoussoukro

who looked after the education of the children. He liked me a great deal, and he gave me a lot of advice, advice necessary to someone like myself, who was being trained to be a chief. But I should say, before going any further, that among the Baoulé people "captivity" was more a word than a fact. The fact that a man was a slave didn't take away from him his value as a human being.'

It was from this slave or captive that the president, as a boy, got a story he never forgot. This was the story. Once upon a time there was a peasant. One year he had a good harvest and he took his crop to market. He sold well, and afterwards he wandered about the market. On a merchant's stall there was a beautiful knife. The peasant fell in love with it and bought it. The peasant cherished his knife. He made a sheath for it, and encrusted the sheath with pearls and shells. One day, when he was pruning a tree, he cut his finger with the knife. In his pain he threw the knife to the ground and cursed it. But then he picked the knife up, wiped off the blood, and put the knife back in the sheath that hung at his side. That was all the story. Why didn't the peasant throw away the ungrateful and wicked knife? It was because of love. The peasant loved his knife. That was the moral.

This was the story the captive at the royal court of Yamoussoukro told the boy who was to be chief. This was the story the president passed on to Hampaté Bâ, the sage, and Hampaté Bâ printed in his book.

Slavery, 'captivity' – so it was an African institution. And, like poison, like sorcery, it continued. But what was the point of the abrupt little story? How could love for a knife translate into brotherly love? The story was in fact a parable – from an old president, an old chief – about power and reconciliation.

Power was the prerogative of the chief; but the good chief, who followed the old ways, also sought reconciliation. Wicked men had been cast aside; but they had once been good and useful and loved; the chief would remember that, and he would forgive.

The benevolent ruler, the ruler seeking the sympathy of the ruled: presented in this way, as an African ideal, the chief became attractive, affecting. I began to enter a little into the African world Arlette saw.

3

Terry's assistant was going to arrange my trip to Yamoussoukro. Arlette was going to put me in touch with an Ivorian at the Institute of Ethno-sociology at the university who had inaugurated a controversial course in 'Drummologie', the science of talking drums. And I had been asking around for a guide to Kilometre 17, where the Evil Spirit had recently been at work, causing a schoolteacher's house to blaze mysteriously from time to time.

These projects began to mature and come together. My days became full and varied. After the random impressions and semi-official meetings and courtesies of the first days, I began to discover themes and people. I began to live my little novel.

Philip – the English expatriate who, with his Guyanese wife, had taken me on the expatriate Sunday excursion to the beach at Grand-Bassam – Philip left a note at my hotel one day. He had found a young Ivorian who would be willing to take me to Kilometre 17 and generally introduce me to African magic. The young man had done some guiding of this sort before, helping a colleague of Philip's with Muslim *marabout* magicians. He was now unemployed – jobs were getting hard to find in the Ivory Coast, even for an Ivorian.

The next morning we all three – Philip leaving his office to act as go-between – met in a grubby little café in the centre of Abidjan.

The young man was well-made, strong, slender and firm at the waist. He had a finely modelled African face, every feature definite, and his skin was very black, a uniform colour, without blotch or tone. He was carefully dressed; his shirt was ironed and clean. I saw him only in this physical way. I couldn't tell whether in his intense eyes there was intelligence, vapidity, a wish to please, or a latent viciousness. His name was Djédjé. He was of the Bété tribe, the second tribe in the Ivory Coast after the Baoulé, to which the president belonged.

Much of our time was spent talking about money, assessing all the expenses that might come up during a visit to the house at Kilometre 17. There would be the taxi – Djédjé was going to arrange that: he knew somebody who would be cheaper than a hotel taxi. There would have to be something for the village chief; something for tips; and there would be Djédjé's fee – he was talking of going to the village beforehand to prepare people.

Djédjé's manner, as he leaned over the coffee cups on the plastic-topped table, was conspiratorial. But it was hard to get him to give a precise figure for anything, even his own fee. An absentness, a troubled lethargy, seemed to come over him when an item was being costed. Philip pressed him gently, never allowing a silence to last too long. It was necessary to fix a limit now, Philip said to me in English. Otherwise, when the time came to pay, Djédjé might grow 'wild' and ask for any amount. It seemed to be settled at the end that the overall price would be between twenty and thirty thousand local francs, thirty-five and fifty pounds. Djédjé was going to telephone me the next day with the final figure, after he had talked with the chief and the taxi-driver.

Djédjé said he was a believer. He meant he believed in the spirits and in the power of magicians; and he said he had agreed to be my guide because he wanted me to be a believer too.

I asked whether there would be any trouble because I was a foreigner. He said no; then he said yes. I was a Hindu, wasn't I? Hindus had a great reputation as magicians, and a *féticheur* might see me as a rival and try to hide things from me. It would be easier for a European, easier for someone like Philip, though Philip and I were the same colour.

This last was an extraordinary thing to say; it was far from being true. But it was true for Djédjé. He still had the tribal eye: people who were not Africans were simply people of another colour.

I asked him to write out his full name for me, and he wrote his family name first, his French Christian name last. When I remarked on the French name, he frowned and made a small, brushing-away gesture with his writing hand. It wasn't important, he said; it was a name he used only in documents.

He telephoned in a message to the hotel desk the next day. '*Le rendez-vous du km 17 est OK.*' And when he came to the hotel he told me that the taxi-driver had fixed the fare at 18,000 francs. I also understood him to say – but his language here was vague, difficult – that a further two thousand would be needed as tips. The taxi-driver was the brother of the village chief, he said. And the chief would need a bottle of whisky: alcohol had 'a special value' for Africans.

He seemed to have kept the price within the limit we had agreed, and I took him to the bar to seal our bargain.

In the dark, 'intimate' hotel bar – rosewood, metal-framed furniture, and buttoned black PVC upholstery – he was as much at ease, or as indifferent to his surroundings, as he had been in the café in the town. Sipping his beer, with the leisure and pauses with which he had drunk coffee in the café, he became conspiratorial again, leaning forward, talking softly, holding me with his intense eyes.

The development of the country had taken a wrong turn, he said. It had begun from the top. What did he mean by that? Not answering my question, but going on to his own concerns, he said that the university was 'saturated'; and there was only one university; and there were stringent rules for entry. And now there was a lot of unemployment. People came to Abidjan and picked up Western ways and for them that was a misfortune. This was another idea. But why was it a misfortune? He lowered his voice, bent closer to me, and said – as though he expected me to understand the full import of what he was saying – that he himself had forgotten how to dance, to do the dances of his tribe, his *ethnie*. In his village he had danced, but in Abidjan he couldn't do the dances.

I asked about his family. He said he had nine sisters and eight brothers. His father was a *planteur*, one of the peasant farmers who had created the wealth of the Ivory Coast, and he had two or three wives. All the children were now in Abidjan. Djédjé himself lived in the house of an uncle, his father's brother. The uncle, a mechanic, had two wives and thirteen children.

I would have liked to hear more of Djédjé's family life, but he wanted to talk about magic. There were Ivorians in Abidjan, he said, who dressed in the modern way and spoke correct French with a French accent. They had lost touch with their *ethnies*, and they said they no longer believed in the African gods. But these people didn't want to go back to the villages because they were afraid of the sorcerers. In their hearts these French Africans believed.

I didn't feel I was understanding all that Djédjé said, and it wasn't a matter of language alone. Perhaps, forgetting his innocence, and misled by his opening statement that the country had taken a wrong turn, I had been looking in his conversation for something that wasn't there: an attitude, a thought-out position. Perhaps – uneducated, unemployed, a villager in Abidjan – he was genuinely confused by the development of the country 'from the top'. Equally, he might only have been trying to get me more interested in the magic to which he had been appointed my guide.

4

One of the names I had been given before coming out to the Ivory Coast was that of Georges Niangoran-Bouah. The note on him said: 'Anthropologist. Contactable at the Institut d'Ethnosociologie at the university. He's around 55, world specialist on "Drummologie", form of communication of tribal drums. Knows African art well, has a fantastic collection of Ashanti weights.'

He sounded quite a figure. And, as often happens when,

as a traveller, I am given the names of important local people, I was shy of getting in touch. But I mentioned his name to various people, and I found out fairly soon that Mr Niangoran-Bouah was academically controversial, that if he was a world expert on Drummologie it was because he had started the subject and had in fact invented the word. Drummologie was apparently as controversial a university course as the one on African philosophy. Some people doubted whether either Drummologie or African philosophy existed.

Arlette, who worked at the university, knew both Niangoran-Bouah and his secretary. The secretary was a fellow *antillaise*, a French West Indian. This lady telephoned me one morning. She had a pecking, fluting voice, and her French – unlike Arlette's – was not easy for me to follow, especially on the telephone. Her name was Andrée, and I understood her to say that her *patron*, Mr Niangoran-Bouah, was still lecturing in the United States, but that I should come to the university to get Mr Niangoran-Bouah's Drummologie book, fresh copies of which had arrived at the office that morning.

The campus was big. Some workmen sitting on the ground below a tree – the crab-grassed ground scuffed down to the roots of the young tree – pointed out the unexpectedly modest, and rather weathered, brick building which was the Institute of Ethnosociology. And it was quite exciting to see, inside, in a corridor hung with name-boards, the little board with the name BOUAH; to enter the little office, and to see the big posters for the course on Drummologie, and another poster with photographs of Ashanti gold weights.

Andrée, the West Indian secretary, Arlette's friend, was a brown woman of more than forty. She was welcoming, but she wasn't like Arlette. She didn't have the vivacity, the size or the softness. Andrée was thinnish, with glasses over strained, big eyes. Her frizzy hair was pulled back tight and done in a bun. She wore a bright blue cardigan and a heavy plaid skirt: the office was air-conditioned. Her style of dress – respectable French, respectable West Indian – proclaimed her as not African. So did the knitting in her bag. She might have knitted the blue cardigan herself. She said – and she clearly had nothing to do in the office that morning – that she liked to keep her hands busy.

Her French was harder for me now than it had been on the telephone. Face to face, she talked faster, in a higher voice, making little rills of sound. I missed half of what she said, and my own poor French, with nothing in the other person's speech to lean on, became worse.

Her desk, with the knitting, was next to the window. She pointed to the big desk of the absent *patron*, next to the corridor wall, and the broad plastic-backed swivel chair behind the desk, and she made me feel the great vacancy in the little room.

But she had the *patron*'s books. She undid a brown paper parcel and gave me a copy of a large-format paperback, *Introduction à la Drummologie*. On the cover there was a photograph of Mr Niangoran-Bouah seated at an open-air drumming and singing ceremony of some sort (with microphones). He was a big man, chieftain-like, draped in African cotton, and he was listening with half-closed eyes to the drums. He acquired a reality for me. He became more than his name and his oddly named subject; his desk became more personal. The little bronze pieces on his desk were indeed things of beauty, as were the gold-weights in the poster on the wall.

A recurring design in those weights – an ideogram or a unit of measure – was the swastika, or something close to it. I asked Andrée whether the weights might have had an Indian origin. I didn't make myself clear. She said only that the weights were very, very old. And that was what the poster said: these objects were old, African, proof of African civilization. To offer proof of African civilization: that, I began to feel, was the cause of the man whose secretary Andrée was.

Andrée, her morning's work done, put her knitting in her bag and locked up the office. She said she would walk with me to where I could get a taxi. As we walked among the students she said, à propos of nothing, that I should take a Nivaquine tablet every day. It was the best protection against malaria. This was something I had thought about doing but not done. She said she would come with me in the taxi to a pharmacy she knew. We went to the pharmacy at the edge of the campus; and it was to Andrée rather than to me that the European or Lebanese pharmacist gave instructions about the Nivaquine.

It was now nearly noon, lunch time. I had taken Andrée far from her office. But she didn't mind. She wanted the company; and I was Arlette's friend. She said she knew a restaurant in the centre.

As we passed the blocks of flats and came out into the main corniche road, Andrée pointed vaguely and said, 'My mother lives there. She reads cards.'

I pretended not to hear.

'My mother's a widow,' Andrée said. 'She reads cards. You should understand. You are a Hindu.'

'Hindus read horoscopes.'

She said, and her speech, clear and precise for the first time, sounded like something from a language lesson: '*Ma . . . mère . . . lit . . . les . . . cartes.*' 'My mother reads cards.'

I said, allowing the taxi to take us further away from where Andrée's mother read cards, 'It's a good gift. A good profession.'

Andrée said sharply, 'My mother's a trained nurse.'

I wondered how Andrée and her mother, both from the island of Guadeloupe in the far-off West Indies, had found themselves in the Ivory Coast. I said, 'Do you live with your mother?' Her voice went high and fluting. She said no. That was how Africans lived, all together. French people, and she meant people like herself, lived independently. I asked how she had come to the Ivory Coast. She said she had met an Ivorian in Paris, and they had married. The marriage had broken up when they came to live in the Ivory Coast.

The restaurant she directed the taxi to in the centre of the town was a big, barn-like building. The doors were open and there were painted menu-boards outside. 'It's clean,' Andrée said, and when we went in – there was as yet no crowd – she said again, 'Isn't it clean?' And it was all right, and there was even a Lebanese in a tie eating fast at one of the tables, head down, jacket on the back of his chair, like a man with a business appointment to keep. But the smell of braised meat and other foods was so high, the air so smoked and oily, even with the doors open, I didn't want to stay. Andrée was disappointed.

We took a taxi to a hotel. It was the only place I knew. It was in a more humid part of town, in a commercial street lined with round-leaved tropical almond trees. There were Lebanese cloth shops, shoe-shine boys, and ragged Africans, most likely foreigners, sitting or lounging on the broken pavement in a smell of sweat. One African, white-capped and in a Muslim gown, was doing his midday prayer, kneeling and bending forward in a private stupor.

The hotel, one of a chain, was of the second rank, a considered blend of flash and shoddiness. But it excited Andrée. She said, 'Expensive,' and her manner improved to match her idea of the place. She gave the taxi-driver a tip on her own account, a fifty-franc piece. And as soon as we were seated in the dining room – next to the glass wall, with a view of the highway below, the black creek, the ships at the far side – she became exacting and French with the uniformed Ivorian waiter, asking precise questions about the menu, taking her time.

The waiter didn't like it. He was used to dealing with European couples, businessmen (there were a few Japanese), solitaries, people grateful for small mercies in unlikely places. Andrée ignored the waiter's exaggerated frowns. She chose; she gave her order. I asked for an omelette. Andrée was abashed. She said what she had chosen was too expensive, and she insisted – the waiter standing by – on changing. She settled for the *jambon* with *frites*.

She was now in a jumpy state, and as soon as the waiter went away she began to talk very fast. She said that life was hard for her. She was trapped in the Ivory Coast, and had no means of returning home – and she meant France, Guadeloupe in the West Indies, left behind many years before, now too far away in every sense. She earned 90,000 francs a month at the university, £150; and she had been lucky, six years before, to get the job. Before that, she had taught at an infants' school. 'Not nice,' she said.

Her marriage to the Ivorian she had met in Paris ended four years after she had come to the Ivory Coast. Her husband's family had broken the marriage up, she said. *Françaises*, Frenchwomen like herself, who married Ivorians should stay in France, she said. In the Ivory Coast the Ivorian families broke the marriages up.

The boy brought the food. He looked pleased with himself. He was carrying six dishes on both arms, as though demonstrating French restaurant style to Andrée, who had been so French with him. She didn't return his smile. She was looking hard and doubtfully at what he was doing. And then – as though doomed by Andrée's stare to fulfil *petit français* ideas about African clumsiness – he dropped one of the six plates. It wasn't one of ours. When, defeated and downcast, he came back to clean up the mess on the carpet, Andrée was eating the *jambon* and *frites* daintily. She left one piece of *jambon* on one side of her plate while she dealt with the other, and it seemed as though she wasn't going to touch the piece of *jambon* she had put to one side. But at the end it had all gone – *frites*, *jambon*, jelly.

She talked again about her life in the Ivory Coast. She didn't take taxis often, she said; they were too expensive. So altogether I was giving her a treat, and I decided to make it as good a treat as the restaurant allowed.

I asked whether she would like cheese. Camembert, gruyère, she asked? I said yes. She said she loved camembert. Didn't she like *chèvre*? Yes, but camembert was the delicacy; and it was something else that was expensive.

She called the boy over, and in her firm way – showing him no compassion after his accident, ignoring and thereby killing the half-surliness with which he tried to fight back – she asked whether they had a variety of cheeses, a choice, a *plateau*. The boy said yes. He began to explain. She cut him short; she ordered him to bring the cheese board. He was recognizing her authority now; and when he brought the board she became very demure, as if rewarding his deference. She took just two little pieces of camembert, though for her *plateau* she could have had four times the quantity.

She said the camembert was good. It wasn't, really. I pressed her to have some dessert. She yielded; she called the boy and asked him to bring the tray with the desserts. She hadn't been abroad, she said, going neatly, without hurry, at the pallid slice of apple tart she had chosen. She hadn't even been to the neighbouring countries, Ghana, Liberia, Guinea. She didn't have the money to travel.

When the bill came she made a delicate attempt at paying, taking out her purse and opening it as though it contained a secret. I made her put the purse away. And then – French graces, West Indian mulatto graces, coming to her after the hotel parody of a French bourgeois lunch – she said she would like to visit me one day in my own country.

We took a taxi back. Andrée said she wanted to get off at the church. But the church, on this occasion at least, was only a marker. Andrée's widowed mother, who read cards, lived near the church, and lived alone, as a Frenchwoman should.

Such solitude, in this bright African light, so like the light of Caribbean afternoons. But how far away home must have seemed to Andrée, who, after Guadeloupe and Paris, now had only the Ivory Coast!

The highway curved on beside the lagoon, through a semi-diplomatic development zone, to the Forum Golf Hotel, opposite the half-developed golf course, where a few old,

thick-trunked baobabs had been allowed to remain, reminders
of tropical forest. In the garden of the hotel, around the
swimming pool, with its artificial rocks, its hollow, plastic
elephants, and its water chute, children played and the topless,
breastless women sunbathed. African guards in brown uniforms sat at various security points. The white sand of what
looked like a beach had been artificially mounded up: the
sand rested on a concrete base, which showed two or three
feet high at the water's edge. It was against this concrete that
the tainted lagoon rocked. On this tainted water there grew
a small, green, cabbage-like plant, with a root like a thin
beard; and these water plants came together in sheltered
places, in the lee of boats, or against sections of the concrete
wall, to form little rocking carpets of living green.

I found, in *Introduction à la Drummologie*, that Andrée was
given a special mention by Mr Niangoran-Bouah: she was
the conscientious *collaboratrice* of a difficult and obstinate
patron. That made him sound attractive. And reading beyond
the acknowledgements, I discovered that Mr Niangoran-
Bouah had indeed made up the word 'drummologie'. Other
words had been thought of – *tamtamologie, tamtalogie, tam-
bourinologie, tambourologie, tambologie, attangbanlogie*. But these
words had been rejected because they seemed to stress the
art of drum-beating rather than the study of the 'talking
drum' as a record of tribal history and tradition. The talking
drum mimicked, and preserved, the actual words of old
chants: these chants were documents of the African past. As
much as the Ashanti weights, with their elements of art and
mathematics, true knowledge of the talking drum gave to
Africa the old civilization which Europeans and colonialists
said didn't exist. This was Mr Niangoran-Bouah's cause.

This was the cause Andrée, from Guadeloupe and France, served.

I told Arlette, when we next met, that I had had great trouble with Andrée's French. Arlette said she had worried about that. Andrée's speech was difficult. Andrée was a little nervous, *un peu nerveuse*. But she was marvellous with her hands. She knitted and made tapestries. Her mother was a very good *voyante*. She read cards and always said interesting things.

Arlette said that Andrée had married again in the Ivory Coast, after the break-up of her first marriage. Her second husband had gone mad. That had had an effect on Andrée's health, and in fact Andrée's mother, a former nurse, had come out to the Ivory Coast to look after Andrée. They didn't live together. But they ate together: every day Andrée had lunch and supper with her mother.

And it was only an hour or so later – this information about Andrée followed by other talk – that Arlette told me that Andrée's second husband had gone mad when he was a political prisoner. He had been badly beaten.

We were walking – Terry Shroeder with us – in the Hotel Ivoire. The Ivoire was more than a hotel. With its bars, restaurants, shops, an area for pin-ball machines, a bowling alley, a skating rink (temporarily defrosted and rejigged into a football field), the Ivoire was the extravagant, air-conditioned fairground of Abidjan. It was a place that people came of an evening to look at and walk in, down the long corridors, and the air-conditioning was so good that many people came dressed against the cold.

Outside, in the warm, along the hotel drive, chasing cars as they arrived, there were prostitutes. So Arlette told me.

(I had missed them; nobody had chased our car.) They were village girls, these prostitutes. More interesting – because it was practised as a sport, rather than out of real need – was student prostitution. Girls at the university didn't sleep with boys at the university. They slept with men in the government, men who had big jobs and could make gifts suitable to a girl who was at the university. It was left to the Abidjan schoolgirls, the *lycéennes*, to sleep with the poor *étudiants*; and since an *étudiant* had only his grant, a *lycéenne* might have an arrangement with two or three *étudiants* at a time, sleeping with each once or twice a week, and collecting her accumulated gratuities at the end of the month.

This kind of behaviour was acceptable because Africans believed in independence in relationships, Arlette said. They didn't look for or expect sexual fidelity. Infidelity as a cause for divorce would be considered frivolous. In a marriage the most important relationship was the relationship between the families. And that was why West Indian women – like Andrée, and like Arlette herself – who married Ivorian men found themselves in trouble when they got to the Ivory Coast. The men simply said goodbye.

Antillaises could be deceived in Paris. They could be dazzled by a man who said he came of a chief's family and had so many slaves and servants – *tant d'esclaves, tant de domestiques* – at home. West Indian women, with their own idea of love, could find in an African's declaration of love and even his offer of marriage things the man never intended. A West Indian woman in the Ivory Coast was without tribe or family; her African husband could, without guilt, say goodbye. If an Ivorian brought home a foreign wife his family chose an African wife for him and sent her to the house. If the

African wife wasn't accepted, the man's family laid a curse on the man. And the man was so terrified of the curse (so terrified, too, of poison) that he usually obeyed.

This was Arlette's story. To live in Africa, she said, was to have all one's ideas and values questioned. And it was good, she added, for that to happen. So, as I had noticed before with Arlette, what seemed like criticism of Africa turned out not to be criticism at all. Arlette, in her own mind, had been re-educated and remade by Africa. Her solitude, as an expatriate, was different from Andrée's.

5

Gil Sherman, Terry Shroeder's assistant, was arranging my trip to Yamoussoukro; and Gil wrote one day that he had found just the man to take me there. The man was Ibrahim Keita. He was the son of a political associate of the president's in colonial times, and he was close to the president. The president wanted to see people playing golf in the Ivory Coast: Ibrahim Keita devoted himself to that cause. He was a keen player and was head of the Golf Federation. He was in charge of the famous golf course at Yamoussoukro. It was also said that he had been entrusted by the president with the general development of Yamoussoukro. He was just the man to show me round. He regularly drove up to Yamoussoukro in his very big and fast Mercedes.

But when I met Ibrahim Keita at Gil Sherman's, he didn't seem to know that he was to take me to Yamoussoukro. He said nothing about it and in fact hardly spoke. French, rather than English, was his international language. He was a big, handsome man of perhaps forty, athletic (and that evening rather tired) from the golf; in colour and features he was a little like Sidney Poitier. His wife, Eileen, was equally reserved that evening. Ibrahim Keita was Muslim; and it is possible that Eileen's reserve was a form of Muslim-African modesty. She was not African, in the strict sense of the word. She had been born in Ghana, but was of West Indian origin, with the family name of Busby: mulatto, middle-class, English-speaking, from the island of Barbados.

Her brother was with her. He too had been born in Ghana, but now he lived in London. He was interested in journalism and African publishing, and was in the Ivory Coast on a short business trip. He was an attractive, bearded brown man, in his thirties. His manner was London and middle-class West Indian; he was bright and good-humoured and open. And it was with him that I talked for much of the evening.

His family story was moving. It was in 1929 that his Barbadian father, after qualifying as a doctor in England, had decided to go and work in Africa. He would have been one of the earliest black professional men from the British West Indies. To someone like that in the 1920s every personal step ahead would have made sharper the feeling of racial deprivation. Slavery had been abolished in the British Empire in 1834; but in the British colonies of the West Indies – neglected, no longer of value – the racial attitudes of both black and white had hardly changed since then. A black professional man in the 1920s would have felt alone, even in his own community.

Dr Busby did what a number of black men like himself talked about but few actually did: he decided to go back to

Africa, to serve Africa, though Africa itself was a colony. He went to the Gold Coast – British-ruled, next door to the French-ruled Ivory Coast – and he worked there until he died.

The Gold Coast became independent Ghana in 1957. Nkrumah ruled, and fell. Now, twenty-five years after its independence, the state of Ghana was in ruins. And Dr Busby's children lived out of the country.

I asked the young man, the doctor's son, what he thought of events in Ghana. He gave an answer that wasn't an answer. He said it was something the country had to go through. But in 1957 – when the Ivory Coast had very little – Ghana was rich, with educated people, and institutions. How had that been squandered? Was it because of Nkrumah – the racialist-socialist ideology, the megalomania, the waste?

The illogicality of the reply surprised me. Nkrumah was a man ahead of his time, young Busby said. *Ahead?* Busby said, 'Have you read Nkrumah's books? You should read his books.' So it was in the words rather than the deeds that the greatness of the man was to be found? Nkrumah, Busby said, had a continental African vision. He was infinitely more than a tribal leader. That continental vision came out in his books, which continued to be revolutionary; and that was why he had built so extravagantly after independence, bankrupting the country. And Nkrumah had done more than anyone for the dignity of black men all over the world. 'Ask any black American,' Busby said.

Gil Sherman was a black American. But he, perhaps diplomatically, didn't hear (he was talking to Ibrahim Keita), and I didn't ask him.

The dignity of the black man – I wanted to pursue that with

Busby. Wasn't that an antiquated idea now? Africa was independent, the black islands of the Caribbean were independent. Weren't there other things for black men to work for?

Busby said, 'Old ideas might turn out to be the best ideas.'

He was a man of faith. He had only the consistency of his racial passion. He was loyal to his father's cause; and after fifty years – though the world had changed – this cause had become like religion. Whatever were the disasters now, black Africa would win through. The world, he said, would still turn to Africa. Illiteracy was soon going to be a problem in England and other Western countries: the world would yet find virtue in African ways. He told an African story, which was like a fable, about a farming community and a boating community who despised one another but, through some ritualized arrangement that preserved the pride of both, yet managed to live together. This was the kind of solution Africa could offer the world.

He lived in England. As a journalist and publisher, he needed England as a base. But this fact, large as it was, played no part in his view of things. I asked him what he wanted for Africa. He said he wanted development. But not the development of the Ivory Coast: he looked for a development which permitted Africans to keep their own soul. He couldn't be more precise. Probably some political objection to capitalism prevented him from seeing how separate French and African ideas were in the Ivory Coast; probably he didn't know how whole the world of Africa still was. Probably, too, the family cause had with him turned to an impossible, religious idea of a pure African way.

He talked to Ibrahim Keita. It was about my trip to Yamoussoukro. And – through my own conversation with somebody else – I heard Keita say (now quite dazed with his golf fatigue) that when you were used to flying a 707 you couldn't take a passenger in a Cessna. It was the first indication I had had that Keita knew about our projected trip to Yamoussoukro. And the message that was coming over was that Keita couldn't take me. There was a problem about the tyres of the Mercedes, and there was apparently no question of a ride with him in the equivalent of a Cessna.

It was a pity about the tyres, Busby said, indirectly giving me the bad news. Ibrahim was a terrific driver; in the Mercedes he could do the 150 miles in two hours. But the replacement tyres Ibrahim had got from Nigeria were not good. Special tyres were needed for a Mercedes of that class, and Ibrahim had had to send to Germany for them.

They left – Ibrahim Keita, Eileen, and her brother. Gil Sherman said he would drive me himself to Yamoussoukro. And during what remained of the evening I heard more about the Mercedes and what nice people the Keitas were.

Andrée, Arlette, young Busby – Africa had called them all, and each had his own Africa. Busby's inherited cause was racial redemption. He needed his mystical faith in Africa. But it was a private cause, from another continent, another past, another way of looking and feeling. A man like Djédjé – my guide to the mysterious blazing house at Kilometre 17 – still knew only about the gods and the tribes. Racially, Djédjé was an innocent.

6

The seventeenth kilometre was on the auto-route to Yamous-soukro. It lay in the soft, ragged countryside beyond the 'popular' African area of Adjamé, beyond the industrial zone. The taxi-driver was, according to Djédjé, the brother of the village chief we were going to see. And, in the half-country beyond the town proper, we stopped at a liquor shop to buy the bottle of whisky which, according to Djédjé, we would have to give the chief.

The shop was a single, rough room. It was basic, even chaste: a few shelves, a few bottles of a particular brand (like samples) on each shelf, a price-tag pinned to each shelf. The shopkeeper, a young man, sat indifferent and cool at a table that was bare except for a shallow, neat pile of old sheets of *Fraternité Matin*. We didn't buy whisky. Djédjé chose a bottle of gin for 3,100 francs, between five and six pounds. The shopkeeper wrapped the bottle in a sheet of *Fraternité Matin*, and Djédjé took the bottle, very carefully.

The land was soft, and the earth seemed stoneless. Trees were tall and scattered, and skeletal – coconuts and palms and the thick-trunked, stubby-branched baobabs. They didn't make a low line of vegetation on the horizon; the eye found only these separate, skeletal, vertical forms.

We turned off the auto-route into a red, unpaved lane, with green bush on either side. It looked as though we had at last got to pure countryside, but orange-coloured Abidjan taxis were bumping along the lane. And soon we passed metal sheds where bananas were stored. Kilometre 17 was not strictly a village; it was a settlement on the edge of Abidjan.

There were no huts; there were only concrete houses. The road, now apparently following an old track, narrowed and twisted between mounds of garbage. But always there were the taxis.

We drove through a banana plantation: the trees in rows, deep drainage canals between the plots of black earth, a protective blue plastic sack over each bunch of growing fruit, the blue a violent, unnatural colour. On other plots, where the trees had borne their fruit and had been cut down to brown stumps, new suckers were growing out of the soft banana trash: a glimpse of the careful agriculture which had made the Ivory Coast rich.

The village we at last came out into had a wide, unpaved main street. The houses, one-storeyed, were of concrete, in bleached and dusty Mediterranean colours. There were many children about, kicking up dust. We stopped in the main street. We got out of the car, entered a narrow passageway between two concrete houses – a sudden sense, after the half-bush, of a town slum – and went into a room from the back. We were in the house of the chief, in his reception room.

Near the window overlooking the street was a set of bulky, plastic-covered, upholstered armchairs. The pea-green walls, grimed and shiny from leaning and touching, were hung, apparently at random, with photographs in passepartout frames. There was a tall bookcase with open shelves: Christian books. The chief was a religious man, not a *pasteur*, but an *évangéliste*.

He came in from another room, tall, middle-aged, with gold-rimmed glasses, a big gold digital wristwatch, rubber sandals, and a big white surgical dressing on a damaged ankle. He wore a patterned chocolate-brown cloth that killed his colour, just as his colour made the cloth look drab and dirty: it was the African taste in fabrics.

Djédjé, grave, his face closed, was carrying the bottle of gin wrapped in the newspaper. The chief's eyes settled on it for a moment and then he didn't look at it; and when we sat on the chairs near the window Djédjé put the bottle behind him on his chair.

People in the street were shouting in through the open window, which was hinged at the top. From time to time, while he talked to us, the chief broke off and shouted to the children, chattering inquisitive faces pushed up between hinged window and window sill, to get away.

People, adults, men, came in through the back door and stood about, near a table strewn with newspapers and various things. Some of the men who came in gave the chief money and he, appearing to pay no attention, held the notes vertically in the closed palm of his left hand. He gestured with this moneyed hand while he talked. From time to time, when he opened his legs, to pat his cloth down between his legs, he showed his dark-blue shorts.

He was clearly pleased with the fame that had come to the village with the affair of the blazing house. But he said that he himself wasn't a believer. He meant he didn't believe in the power of sorcery, being a Christian and an evangelist. (On the wall above his chair there was a photograph of him in a suit receiving a diploma or certificate when he had been made an evangelist.) There had never been any trouble in the village, he said, no spiritual or magical manifestation, no sign of the Evil Spirit. But then this thing had begun to happen in the compound of the school. The house of one of the teachers,

Mr Ariko, had begun to catch fire. And that was an undoubted manifestation.

Of course the matter had been brought to his attention and he, as village chief, had made investigations. He discovered that Mr Ariko had two wives. Mr Ariko had not long before given money to both wives – 40,000 francs to each, about £70. But the second wife thought she had been given less than the first wife. That was what the chief had found out, and the case at that stage had seemed perfectly straight-forward: the second wife, or the Evil Spirit within her, had 'provoked' the fires. It was a simple enough matter, and there were ways of dealing with it.

There was a prophet in Bingerville, the old French colonial settlement not far from Abidjan. The prophet was quite well known and had a little sect of his own. He was consulted, and he prepared a white powder, which he gave to the chief. The powder was to be placed on the feet of the second, dis-affected wife; it was guaranteed to destroy whatever magical powers she had been invested with by the Evil Spirit.

This was done. The second wife became ordinary again. But the fires continued in Mr Ariko's house. The problem was extraordinary. It began to drive everyone to distraction. Muslim *marabouts* and other magicians were brought in to try their hand. The tormented Mr Ariko was spending a lot of money. Sacrifices were made. But nothing happened. Then an evangelist of the Celestial Christian sect offered his ser-vices. The Celestial Christians were a new group, from Ghana; they had been in the Ivory Coast for only three years and were anxious to make their mark. The chief decided to let the Celestial Christian evangelist try.

The evangelist – who had a pretty shrewd idea of what was

going on – watched the house. He saw that during the night a young girl, physically invisible, was moving freely in and out of the house. It was that girl, and no one else, who was doing the mischief. In the morning the Celestial Christian evangelist assembled all the young girls from the school compound. He went straight to the young girl who had made herself invisible during the night: she was the daughter of the second, disaffected wife. She confessed, and her story could scarcely be believed: the gift of sorcery had been passed on to her by her mother, before her mother's own powers had been destroyed by the prophet's white powder.

The Evil Spirit had been especially devious at Kilometre 17. It was that passing on of the sorcerer's gift that had baffled everybody. And that was why the case had caught the public imagination.

Powder had been put on the girl's feet, and she and her mother had been packed off to the mother's village. The other wife, out of simple prudence, had also been sent back to her village. Since then, the chief said, there had been no trouble at all.

The chief said reflectively, clutching the banknotes: 'I tell you that there had been no trouble in the village before this business. But I think I should tell that in this area we do in fact have some well known *génies*.' Djinns, spirits. 'Did you notice that very sharp bend in the road? Near the banana plantation. There are some *génies* at that corner. Very small hens.' He made a little gesture with both hands. 'Not chickens, but very small hens. If a driver sees them he is bound to have an accident.'

I wondered about the wife and the daughter who had been sent back to the village. Would they remain sorcerers? It was possible, the chief said. And Djédjé, always more grave than the chief, said that in the village – far from good prophets and Celestial Christians – the power of the white powder could be annulled, *annulé*. How did people become sorcerers? The terrible gift could be passed on to them when they were children. It could be passed on to anyone; there was no question of personal wickedness.

Djédjé said, 'Without civilization, everyone would be a sorcerer.'

It was his vision of chaos, a world without reason or rules. I thought I understood that. But then I wasn't sure I knew what Djédjé meant by civilization. When we had last met he had spoken against 'development from the top'. He pined for village ways, the dances of his *ethnie*; he believed in fetishes. Was civilization the sum of those old, true things: an organized society, worshipping correctly, having access to the magic that protected it from arbitrary evil? Or was Djédjé saying something simpler? Was he, in the presence of the chief, a government official, repeating the government's case for 'development'?

It was time for the chief to get his bottle of gin. He took the newspaper-wrapped bottle and, casually, half unwrapped it to check the label. His sour, care-burdened face momentarily looked fulfilled; and then, making purely social conversation, as if offering us a little extra in return for our gift, he grumbled for a bit about the difficulties of getting labour for his fields. People preferred to work for white men, foreigners from the big companies, who of course could afford to pay more.

On the table at the other end of the room was the copy of *Fraternité Matin* with the story about the burning house.

Djédjé asked for the newspaper; the chief graciously gave it. And as we drove on in the taxi to the house itself – the chief had cleared our visit, and one of the young men who had come to the room was keeping us company – Djédjé read the newspaper story, ceaselessly fingering the paper, as though the type was raised.

He shook his head. He gave a short, wise laugh. He said, 'The Celestial Christians are certainly making publicity with their success.'

The schoolteacher's house was one of a cluster of little low concrete houses, all ochre-coloured and flat to the ground. The settlement – so ordinary, though so famous – was still a living place. But in the middle of its midday life there was mystery. The door of the schoolmaster's house was open; the front room was apparently empty. Outside the open door, and set firmly in the earth, was a wooden cross, about three feet high, with the metal crucifix of the Celestial Christians.

Each house in the settlement had its own open cooking shed at the back. The soft red earth between the sheds and houses had been swept and showed rake marks. Wood fires between stones burned below aluminium pots. One girl was sweeping up wet, nasty-looking rubbish with a broom made from the ribs of long coconut leaves. A few feet away a woman was using a pestle to grind aubergines in a little bowl set on the ground; and there was a neat child's turd near by.

There were little children everywhere. Some were rolling about playfully on a purple-patterned grass mat. Djédjé, translating what our official guide said, told me they were the children of the teacher. But the guide was wrong, or Djédjé had misunderstood him. The teacher's child was a melancholy little fellow, sitting alone and still, like a little old man, beside a cooking fire. Tears had stained his dusty face; he had fresh tears in his eyes. Sorcery was no joke; it had come here as a family disaster. The boy was being looked after by the sister of the teacher, now that the teacher's wives had been sent back to their villages. The sister, squatting beside her fire, was in a green African dress. It was only when she stood up I saw that she herself was very young.

The land rose up sharply at the back of the cooking sheds. It was planted with banana trees and other trees. Scattered there, like rubbish, were some of the partly burnt things from the teacher's house, scorched clothes, scorched furniture. Disappointing to me – I had expected evidence of bigger blazes. But these scorched small objects, though discarded as malignant things, were still on display. The mystery was still fresh, its relics (already legendary) still accessible.

In a cooking shed at the end of the row a group of women and girls – to get a little of the visitors' attention – was encouraging a small child to dance. They chanted, clapped and laughed, and they looked from the child to us. And the toddler did for a few moments break into a slow, sweet, stamping dance: his feet alive, his legs alive, his child's face mournful and blank. The women and girls laughed. The child did another little dance. It was done for us, but there was no answering wave from the women to our wave of farewell.

We drove around the area. The bush, or what had looked like bush, had surprises. All around the settlement with the teacher's house (and the cross) were the buildings of a research institute of some sort. Many Europeans were about. I expressed surprise. The man with us as our official guide (he was the son of a former chief) resented my surprise. He spoke sharply to me, as to a foreigner and a fool; and he never returned to good humour. We set him down at the main road, the Yamoussoukro auto-route. His dark African cloth quickly turning him all black, he crossed with a stamping swagger to the township on the other side and was at once lost in the crowd.

7

The Djédjé business ended badly. The fault was mine. I gave him too much money. He had said that he wanted 2,000 francs for tips. I hadn't understood that this – less than £4 – was his own modest fee. I gave him that; and added 6,000 francs, £10, as his fee. His eyes popped. With the first violent or inelegant gesture I had seen him make he grabbed the notes I offered. And then, slightly stooped, as though arrested in the grabbing gesture, he trembled for a second or two with excitement.

He telephoned early the next morning. He said he was going to come in the afternoon to take me to a famous *féticheur* in Bingerville.

He came. When I went down to meet him in the hotel lobby he said he had forgotten to tell me in the morning that the *féticheur*'s fee for an *expérience* would be 15,000 francs. I said I didn't want an *expérience*; I just wanted to talk to the *féticheur*. Djédjé said it was a big *expérience*. The *féticheur* would cut his hand with a knife and make the wound close up again.

Djédjé said, 'For 15,000 francs he will give you three *expériences*.'

'How much for one?'

'Perhaps 5,000 will be enough.'

We went out to the hotel forecourt. He hadn't arranged a taxi this time; I thought he had. He asked me to sit in one of the hotel taxis. He stood outside with the driver and they began a palaver. It went on for a while. Djédjé's manner changed. He ceased to be grave. His body became looser; he propped himself in varying postures against the taxi and laughed and chattered like a street-corner lounger. I looked out of the window, to hurry things up. Djédjé, laughing and casual, as though he knew me very well, asked me to wait.

At last he and the driver got into the taxi, and we started. The driver didn't put the meter on. I took this to mean that the fare to Bingerville had been settled. But it hadn't, because after a mile or two the driver raised the subject. He said to me, 'You will have no trouble getting a taxi back from Bingerville.' I asked Djédjé what they had arranged about the fare. Djédjé said the taxi-driver had asked for 10,000 francs, and he had offered the driver a thousand. I took this to mean that some mid-way price was expected.

I said, 'Would we be able to get a taxi back?'

Djédjé said, 'Taxis are hard to get at Bingerville.'

He began to talk about the powers of *féticheurs*. There was an even more famous one than the one we were going to see, but he had asked an astronomical price. That particular *féticheur* could make himself invisible and go through a closed door. It would have been a good *expérience* for me, but it wasn't worth the money.

The taxi-driver interrupted and spoke for some time in an African language.

I asked, 'What's he saying?'

Djédjé said, 'He wants 15,000 francs.'

'But that's absurd.'

'That's what I told him. I offered him 5,000 for the trip out and 5,000 for the trip back.'

'So you've settled for the original 10,000?'

'Yes.'

It was very high, but there was no question of getting out of the taxi. It was mid-afternoon, very hot, and so far on the road out of Abidjan I hadn't seen another taxi. I said, 'Tell him that is to include an hour's waiting.'

It seemed settled, at last.

The highway to Bingerville cut through soft slopes of bush: a wide view, the lower sky hazy in the heat.

Djédjé talked about fetishes. They could be very expensive, he said. Europeans often wanted fetishes. I remembered that in Djédjé's eyes I was like a European. I said I didn't want a fetish; I only wanted to talk to the *féticheur*.

'Yes, yes,' Djédjé said, not believing a word. 'Some Europeans, some Africans too, can pay up to 100,000 francs for a fetish.'

The taxi-driver said, 'Listen. About my fare – '

I said, 'That's settled.'

And Djédjé with an open palm made a silencing gesture at the driver.

Bingerville appeared, a scatter of ochre-coloured concrete buildings on low hills: like Grand-Bassam, another early French settlement in the Ivory Coast: degraded colonial architecture, concrete and corrugated iron, at the limit of empire.

Djédjé had said he had made arrangements with the *féticheur*. It turned out now that he didn't know where the *féticheur* lived.

We turned off into a dirt road. It soon became a track. We asked directions of a plump young man who was wearing an orange-coloured tee shirt printed *Bingerville*. He was all good nature. He was perfectly ready to direct strangers to the local *féticheur*.

We got back on to the highway. And Djédjé, to cover up his mistake, told of a particularly powerful fetish that had been prepared by the *féticheur* for a deputy of the national assembly at the last elections. The fetish converted votes given for the deputy's opponent into votes for the deputy. The deputy won by a big margin, and the deputy's opponent went mad wondering what had happened to all the votes that had been promised him.

We got lost for the second time. And again, this time stopping near a group of schoolchildren in uniform, we had to ask – or Djédjé had to ask, calling out of the window – where the house of the *féticheur* was. And again no one seemed put out or surprised by our inquiry. One man – stopped as he was walking busily by – not only told us where the house was, but also offered (as though he hadn't really been going anywhere) to be our guide. He got into the seat beside the driver and at once became very cheerful, relishing the idea of even a short ride.

The turning we wanted was unmarked. It was a track across waste ground, and it led past a ragged screen of trees and bushes to a village: abrupt life in what, from the road, had looked only like bush. There seemed to be no road at all in the village. We drove straight at houses, and the car turned between houses. Dusty yards opened into dusty, littered yards, one man's back yard somebody else's front yard: cooking fires, wood piles, cooking utensils on black, trampled earth, children, men and women in a variety of costumes: the relaxed afternoon life of the village.

We were just a minute or two from the splendid highway, with its logic of straight lines and easy curves. But already we were in an older and more tangled world, a version of a forest settlement. We continued to drive between houses. It continued to seem that we wouldn't be able to get round the corners, that we would have to stop. But we didn't stop.

Djédjé, getting more tense as we drove deeper into the village, said suddenly, 'You changed money? Give me some thousand-franc notes. It would be better, the thousand-franc notes.'

My money was in a side pocket of my trousers. I was sitting, and couldn't pull out the notes one by one. I pulled out what the bank at the hotel had given me: a set of ten new thousand-franc notes.

Djédjé said, 'That's ten thousand, isn't it? Give me ten thousand.'

But he had told me that five thousand would be enough for the *féticheur*, for one *expérience*.

I was uneasy at getting deeper in the village, which seemed to go on and on. And I was so uncertain now of Djédjé and the taxi-driver, who had changed their minds about every agreement, that I decided to give up the journey.

I said to the driver, 'Go back to Abidjan. Go back to the hotel.'

He had enjoyed the drama of taking his car between the houses. Now, stylishly, making a lot of dust, he turned in somebody's yard, and we twisted back through the village to the waste ground and the asphalt road. We bumped down into the road.

Just at that moment Djédjé shouted, 'Stop!'

The driver stamped on the brake. Djédjé bent forward once, twice. He said, 'I have a bad conscience about this.' He began to rock backward and forward in his seat. He said again, 'I have a bad conscience about this.'

The driver looked from Djédjé to me. The village and the *féticheur*, or Abidjan and the hotel?

I said, 'The hotel.'

We dropped our passenger – glad to get out of the car now – and went on to the highway. We drove for a mile or so: the bush, the black highway, the hot afternoon glow.

Djédjé said with passion, 'Everything the *féticheur* does will be at my expense. At my expense.'

Nothing was said to the driver. But he pulled in at the side of the highway.

Djédjé said, 'You are making me feel badly. You are making me feel badly.' His eyes went red; sweat broke out on his forehead. He was rocking himself again. I thought he was going to have a fit.

He said, 'You see how I am sweating. You believe I was deceiving you. You make me feel badly. Everything I did, I did for you. I asked you for the money only to protect you. If the *féticheur* had seen a European pull out all those notes he would have asked for a lot of money. That was why I asked you for the ten thousand francs in thousand-franc notes.'

The taxi-driver, always cool, said to Djédjé, 'None of this alters my fare, you understand. He will have to settle my bill.'

I said, 'The hotel.'

We drove back in silence, until Djédjé said, 'Tomorrow. Come to town tomorrow. I will take you to a *féticheur* in town. He wouldn't do anything for you especially. He will be giving a display. You will see it free.'

And that was what he said again when he followed me into the hotel lobby.

I felt foolish, drained, sad. I felt Africa as a great melancholy – that expensive highway, with its straight lines and curves; that village, with its antique, forest squalor and its *féticheur*; Djédjé's belief, his exaggerated emotions, his changes of personality.

Without civilization, Djédjé had said the day before, everybody would be a sorcerer.

8

To be black was not to be African or to find community with Africans. Many West Indian women who had married Africans had discovered that. So Janet told me. West Indian women, whatever their background, were house-proud; they found Africans dirty. And then there was the problem with the African families. Janet had heard versions of the story Arlette had told: the African family choosing an African wife for the man and sending this wife to the house, with the threat of a curse if she was rejected.

It was easier for a white woman to marry an African, Janet thought. The white woman would know she was marrying exotically; that would be part of the attraction. The

West Indian woman, with her own racial ideas, would be looking in Africa for a double security.

Janet herself was black. She had grown up in England, where her Guyanese family had settled. She was blessed with great beauty (tall, slender, long-necked), and she had the security of her beauty. She had no anxieties about 'belonging'. Happily removed from the political nastiness of independent Guyana, she spoke of herself as someone 'from England'. She had come out to the Ivory Coast with her English husband Philip. Philip had spent most of his working life in Africa, and it was one of his sayings that in their mixed marriage Janet was the English partner; he was the African.

At dinner in a rough but well-known beach restaurant (Philip and Janet were great restaurant-goers), and later over coffee in their flat in the centre of Abidjan (the black lacquer furniture in the big sitting room from London, from Habitat), Philip told me how he had come out to Africa.

Just after he had left school, in Scotland, he 'discovered' the motor-car. Motor-cars became his obsession; he wanted to be a racing driver. Soon enough it came to him that he wasn't making any money from driving. So he enrolled as a trainee teacher in a programme run by a British government department concerned with overseas development. The trainees were sent out to East Africa, and East Africa was attractive to Philip, not only because of the sun and the easy life, but also because it was the territory of the great motor rally, the East African Safari.

There were forty trainees in Philip's year. They could be divided into four groups. There were those, about ten or twelve, who wanted to go out to Africa to convert the Africans to Christianity. There were a few, from very rich families, who were moved by the idea of charity. There were those who went to Africa to get away from personal distress, emotional entanglements. The fourth, and largest, group went out for the sun and the easy life. Philip belonged to this group. And it was people from this group who lasted; most of the others cracked within the first year and gave up Africa.

But the Uganda that Philip went out to soon became another place. Idi Amin, the former army sergeant, took over. Philip was having lunch one day in a little English-run restaurant in Kampala when Amin came in, just like that, without ceremony. This caused a stir; and Amin added to the excitement by paying the lunch bills of everybody who was then in the restaurant. Philip said, 'So I can say Amin bought me lunch.' On another occasion Amin appeared, again without warning, at a rugby match in which a representative Uganda team was playing. He stood in the back of his Land-Rover and watched, shouting, 'Come on, Uganda!' Later he bought beer for all the players. This was how he was in the early days, the army man, grand of gesture, immensely popular with the expatriates, and quite different from the tribal politicians he had displaced. Then he had become more tribal than any, and he had drenched Uganda in blood.

I had spent some months in Uganda in 1966, at the time of an earlier coup. Philip, answering an inquiry of mine, said, 'Many of the young people you knew would have been killed.'

This was the Africa Philip had worked in. Events had carried him along. He had moved from contract to contract, country to country. He spoke calmly about Uganda; he had trained himself to that calm. He was still trying to arrive at a larger attitude. And now, I felt, he was touched by Janet's own detachment from Africa.

African countries, whatever their political horrors, genuinely valued education, Philip said. That gave meaning to whatever he had done. In England, he said, education had ceased to be valued. Once, when he was in London between contracts, he had taught at a comprehensive school. He had been shocked by the illiteracy and indifference of the students; one boy, dazzled by his contract with a football club, left the school absolutely without any training. Still, Philip liked England. It remained a good place, if not to work in, then to work from. He and Janet were negotiating to buy a house in London: he had photographs to show.

He had become an expatriate, a man out of his country, a man moving between two continents: one place always made bearable by the prospect of departure for the other.

About Djédjé – to whom he had introduced me – Philip wasn't surprised. He had from the beginning feared that Djédjé would grow 'wild'. And it was Philip's job at that moment – in the inter-state African organization for which he worked – to deal with high African officials who were going 'wild', but on an astronomical scale, and were coming hotfoot to Abidjan to ask for millions. There was a way of dealing with this wildness without causing offence, Philip said. You asked questions, and more questions; you became technical. The official finally couldn't answer, and calmed down.

The flat where we were was high up in a high block. Tropical Ivory Coast rain had found a gap between the concrete and the metal frame of the sitting-room window and discoloured the wall. That nagged Janet. She said, 'There is no maintenance.' And I thought I saw in the discoloured wall the origin of something Philip had said when he had first driven me round the splendours of Abidjan. He had said, 'Africa seeps through.' I didn't know him then. I had seen him as a man with an African cause, and I had thought the comment was one of approval: Africa humanizing and softening the brutalism of industrial civilization. But he meant only what Janet said: there was no maintenance.

There was another side to that. In Africa, Philip said, distress came to those who cared more about Africa than Africans did, or cared differently. In the Ivory Coast, was there really virtue in maintaining what had been given? Was there a finality about the model?

He had come to Africa for the sun and the good life. Now Africa had become the starting point for speculation. He had become more thoughtful than he might have done if he had stayed in England; he had become more knowledgeable and more tolerant. And simply by being in Africa, he – like other expatriates I met – now took a special conscientiousness to his job. He had become a good man.

Yet men, especially in Africa, had to know why they did things. And – as I had felt after my talk with Busby – in Africa this issue could still only be left in the air.

9

In the morning I was telephoned from the hotel lobby by a man called Ebony. He said he had heard from Busby that a writer was in Abidjan, and he had come to meet this writer. He, Ebony, was himself a poet.

I went down to see him. He was a cheerful young man of regal appearance, with the face of a Benin bronze, and he was regally attired, with a brightly patterned skull-cap and a rich African tunic. He said the skull-cap and tunic were from Volta. His family employed labourers from Volta and he had always, even as a child, liked their clothes.

He had been a journalist, he said, but he had given it up, because in the Ivory Coast journalism was like smoking: it could damage your health. He liked the joke; he made it twice. But he was vague about the journalism he had done. He said he was now a government servant, in the department of the environment. He had written a paper on things that might be done environmentally in the Ivory Coast. But after twelve months he had heard nothing about his paper. So now he just went to the office and from time to time he wrote poetry.

He said, 'I have a theory about African administrations. But it is difficult and will take too long to tell you.'

He had come to see me – and the hotel was a good way out of the town – because he was sociable; because he wanted to practise his English; and because, as a poet and intellectual, he wanted to try out his ideas.

I offered coffee. He offered me a cola nut, the African token of friendship. I nibbled at my grubby, purple-skinned nut: bitter. He chewed his zestfully, giving little dry spits of chewed husk to his left and right, and then at the end of his chew taking out the remainder of the husk with his fingers and placing it on the ashtray.

He asked why I had come to Ivory Coast. I said because it was successful and French.

He said, 'Charlemagne wasn't my ancestor.'

I felt it had been said before, and not only by Ebony. He ran on to another idea. 'The French run countries like pig-sties. They believe that the sole purpose of men is to eat, to go to the toilet and to sleep.' So the French colonialists created bourgeois people. Bourgeois? 'The bourgeois want peace, order. The bourgeois can fit into any political system, once they have peace. On the other hand, the British colonialists created entrepreneurs.' Entrepreneurs? 'Entrepreneurs want to change things.' Entrepreneurs were revolutionaries.

Antithesis, balance: the beauty rather than the validity of a thought: I thought I could detect his French training. I began to examine his ideas of the bourgeois and the entrepreneur, but he didn't encourage me. He said, playfully, it was only an idea.

Starting on another cola nut – he had a handful in his tunic pocket – he said, 'Africans live at peace with nature. Europeans want to conquer or dominate nature.'

That was familiar to me. I had heard similar words from young Muslim fundamentalists in Malaysia: ecological, Western romance bouncing back like a corroborating radio signal from remote, inactive worlds. But that again was an idea Ebony didn't want to stay with.

Ebony said, 'I saw white men for the first time when I was fourteen or fifteen, when I went to school. That was the first time I discovered the idea of racial superiority. African children are trained not to look elders in the eye. It is disrespectful. At school the French teachers took this to be a sign of African hypocrisy.'

What was the point of this story?

Ebony said, 'So I thought my French teachers inferior.'

I felt this racial story, with its triumphant twist, had previously had a sympathetic foreign listener. And it turned out that there was a Scandinavian woman journalist who had made a great hit with Ebony. She was now in Spain and Ebony earnestly asked me – two or three times – to look her up and pass on his regards.

Ebony said, 'When my father sent me to the school, do you know what he said? He said, "Remember. I am not sending you to the school to be a white man or a Frenchman. I am sending you to enter the new world, that's all." '

I felt that in his own eyes Ebony had done that. He had made the crossing more easily than Djédjé. Ebony said he had no money, no car. The salary he got from the government was less than the rent he paid. He had come to the hotel on his bicycle. But I thought he was relaxed, a whole man. He knew where he was, how he had got there, and he liked the novelty of what he saw. There was no true anxiety behind his scattered ideas. At any rate he was less anxious than a romantic or concerned outsider might have wished him to be. Ideas about Africa, words, poetry, meeting foreigners – all this was part of his relishing of life, part of his French-inspired role as intellectual, part of the new world he had happily entered.

He went away on his bicycle, and I took a taxi later to a beach restaurant at the end of the city, beyond the industrial and port area. The lunch there, and the French style of the place, was usually worth the fare and the journey in the midday heat through the traffic and the crowds. But today it wasn't so.

It was more than a matter of an off-day. The waiters, impeccable the day before, were casual, vacant. There were long delays, mistakes; some of the portions were absurdly small; the bill, when it came, was wrong. Someone was missing, perhaps the French or European manager. And with him more than good service had gone: the whole restaurant-idea had vanished. An elaborate organization had collapsed. The waiters – Ivorian: these jobs were lucrative – seemed to have forgotten, from one day to the next, why they were doing what they did. And their faces seemed to have altered as well. They were not waiters now, in spite of their flowered tunics. Their faces and manners radiated various degrees of tribal authority. I saw them as men of weight in the village: witch-doctors, herbalists, men who perhaps put on masks and did the sacred dances. The true life was there, in the mysteries of the village. The restaurant, with its false, arbitrary ritual, was the charade: I half began to see it so.

Ebony had been told by his father: 'I am not sending you to the school to become a white man. I am sending you to enter the new world.'

The new world existed in the minds of other men. Remove those men; and their ideas – which after all had no finality – would disappear. Skills could be taught. What was fragile – to men whose complete, real life lay in another realm of the spirit – was faith in the new world.

It was in this unsettled mood that at last, on the public holiday that marked the independence of the Ivory Coast, I went with Gil Sherman to the president's ancestral village of Yamoussoukro.

10

The auto-route went through a soft green land, and then through forests where grew the irreplaceable hardwoods that had given the economy a start. (Mighty trunks, just two or three or four at a time, chained on to heavy lorries on the road: mighty log piles on the timber docks – with a bustling dockers' settlement – in an oily black creek in Abidjan: the logs then chained again, and swung one or two at a time into the holds or on to the stripped decks of vessels with foreign, far-off names.) The country was organized; it was a country at work; and the money had spread down. Money had come to the people of bush and forest, and their villages were now built in concrete. In one small town where we stopped for a while there was even a parody of a modern hotel.

After 150 miles – regularly marked off in kilometres – we came to Yamoussoukro. The road rose. At the top, quite suddenly, it was like an airport runway in a cleared wilderness. Lamp standards lined the broad avenue on either side. In the distance was the twelve-tiered tower of the Hotel President, lifting above itself, to one side, two octagonal slabs of concrete (with the tower restaurant between the slabs), like a giant sandwich with the corners cut away. Towards that we drove: landscaped grounds, gardens, a white marble entrance, a lobby in red and chocolate marble, mirrors set in the chamfered angles of the marble pillars. The upholstered chairs were in virulent blue and green, not restful.

The room I was given was opulent. The bathroom fittings staggered. It was very cold: the air-conditioning was fierce.

I turned the system off, but the room never lost its chill while I was there. The great window, of very thick glass, was sealed. It gave a view of the enormous swimming pool, around which, on a wide paved area, lounge chairs were set in a larger circle.

Beyond that, and beyond the buildings of the older Hotel President (Yamoussoukro had never ceased to grow), was parkland: parkland created out of the African bush. It was the famous golf course, landscaped, with planting: a foreign eye had drawn out the picturesque possibilities of what to an African would have been only bush. The mist in the distance looked – to me – like the heat mist on the banks of the Congo river. But Yamoussoukro was cooler than the coast, and this was the mist of the harmattan, the cool, sand-charged wind that blew all the way down from the Sahara at this season.

It was a great creation, the golf course, perfection in a way. It represented prodigious labour. Yet it was only a view: one look took it all in. And soon it wasn't enough. Splendour on this scale, in this setting, and after a 150-mile drive, only created an appetite for more: the visitor began to enter the ambition and fantasy of the creator. There was a main street, very wide; there was a market; there were workers' settlements. Something like a real town was attaching itself to the presidential creation. But the visitor, always quickly taking for granted what had been created, continued to be distracted by the gaps, the scarred earth, the dusty vacancies. And, if you didn't want to play golf, there was nothing to do.

There were the president's crocodiles. They were to be fed at five. The presidential palace was some distance away, down one of the great avenues. Gil Sherman's car was necessary. In the levelled land, in the glare and emptiness of the afternoon, the scale of everything seemed magnified. The palace wall went on and on. Beside it was a lake. In the middle, an iron-railed causeway lined with young coconut trees led to a palace gate, guarded by soldiers of the presidential guard in maroon-coloured tunics. The cars of visitors – mainly white – were parked on the causeway.

In the lake on either side were the crocodiles. We saw the first just as we left the car: barely noticeable in the muddy water, a mere protuberance of eyes, until its thorny back became clear. We exclaimed. An African, possibly an official (from his lounging, casual stance), said, '*Il est petit*'. A small one. Then we saw eyes and thorny backs everywhere on the surface of the water – the thorns like the thorns on the bark of the baobab tree.

On one side of the causeway there was a stone-paved embankment sloping down to the water. On this embankment were a number of crocodiles, small ones, absolutely still, eyes bright and apparently unseeing, jaws open, the lower jaw of each crocodile showing only as a great hollow, oddly simple in shape, oddly clean and dry-looking, yellow-pink and pale. Flies moved in and out of those open jaws. On the other side of the causeway there was no paved embankment, only a sandy bank, marked by the tails of crocodiles. White feathers, as of a chicken, were scattered about in the sand. There were crocodiles on the bank. They were like the colour of the sand and from a distance were not noticeable.

The feeder was already in attendance. He had come in a grey Land-Rover; it was parked on the causeway. He was clearly a special man. He was very tall, very thin. He wore a skull-cap and a flowered gown. He had an official with him, a man of more ordinary size in a grey, short-sleeved safari suit. In one hand the feeder had a thin, long knife; in his other hand he had a tin or bucket with pieces of meat. Heart or lungs, Gil Sherman told me: pale pink, with bits of animal 'piping'.

The feeder made a rattling sound on the iron rails. Then he threw the meat. The crocodiles on the paved embankment were awkward, slow. They had to tilt their long snouts against the flat paving stones – showing the pale-yellow underside of their bodies – to pick up the meat. They couldn't get the meat that had fallen on their own backs or into the crevices between the paving stones. They didn't seem always to know where the meat had fallen.

While the feeder threw the meat, the grey-suited official with him clucked and called softly to the crocodiles, speaking to them as to children. *'Avalez, avalez.'* 'Swallow, swallow.'

Later, on the the other side of the causeway, there was another ritual. The older, bigger crocodiles were there, yellow, with twisted snouts, heavy bellies, and teeth which, when closed together, suggested a long, jagged, irregularly stitched wound.

The tall feeder was now holding a black chicken by the wings. He swung the chicken slowly up and down. The squawks of alarm from the chicken died down. The chicken lost control of its neck, which hung limp. Two old crocodiles, as though used to the ritual, waited close together on the sand. More meat was thrown and gobbled up, except where it had fallen on the backs of the crocodiles. Turtles, appearing in the water, swam ashore for their meat. One young crocodile, having got his meat, swam away fast to a little sand-bank on the lake to eat or ingest his meat without disturbance. Then the chicken was thrown at the two old crocodiles. The open jaws snapped shut. The crowd gasped. But the feeder hadn't thrown straight; and the crocodiles hadn't moved. The stunned chicken fluttered its wings; it partly recovered from its stupor; it ran along to the end of the sandy bank, near the causeway.

The tall feeder in the flowered gown didn't allow the chicken to get away. He jumped over the rail to the bank and – his long thin knife his only means of defence – walked unhurriedly past the crocodiles to where the chicken was. The chicken didn't run. The feeder seized it, climbed back over the rail to the road. And again the ritual swinging of the bird by the wings was accompanied by clucking calls to the two waiting crocodiles from the grey-suited official. Again the bird was thrown. Again the jaws snapped; again the bird escaped. But now the clucking calls had brought from the water on to the sand a crocodile even bigger and older than the other two. His snout was battered at the tip. His teeth looked stained and old and worn. The chicken's limp neck was placed on the iron rail; the feeder began to bring down his knife. I didn't look.

A shout from the crowd told me that the chicken had been thrown. And when I turned I saw the bird turned to a feathery debris in the seemingly grinning maw of one croco-dile, not the oldest, round unseeing eyes apparently alight with pleasure, black feathers sticking out on either side of the jaw. A moment's ingestion, and all was gone, except for a mash in the lower jaw. The ceremony was over. The feeder, skull-capped, prettily gowned, took his tin and walked back, unsmiling, to the Land-Rover.

A public ceremony of kingship outside the big blank wall of the presidential palace. Behind that wall there were trees, and somewhere among those trees was the president's ancestral village with the old palaver tree. That site, which felt sacred now, the scene perhaps of more private rituals, was not open to the public. Ibrahim Keita, the golfer, the president's protégé, the man said to be charged by the president with the development of Yamoussoukro, Ibrahim had seen the village behind the palace wall. But Ibrahim's West Indian wife hadn't.

Ibrahim was to have guided me around Yamoussoukro. But he hadn't been able to do that. He had, however, done a gracious and unexpected thing: he had deputed his elder brother to show Gil Sherman and me around. The brother came in the morning to the Hotel President. The brother was a doctor, smaller than Ibrahim, softer, grey-haired, with glasses, and with the confident manner of some black West Indian professional men of established family.

The Keita family was from the neighbouring state of Guinea; in the Ivory Coast they were refugees of a sort. And the doctor's story that morning, in the marble lobby of the Hotel President, was of his escape from Guinea in 1964. A quiet hint from someone, a false message to an official, an early-morning drive across the border: Dr Keita still marvelled at his escape, was still shocked by the terrors of Guinea, where in 1964 people like himself, professional men, educated men, men of the *cheferie*, were being picked up and killed 'like cattle', locked in cells and left to die, without food or water: the famous 'black diet' of Guinea.

Just across the border, in a climate like this, among people like those one saw, there was that kind of African kingship.

It gave an added wonder to Yamoussoukro, to the chieftaincy or kingship symbolized by the crocodiles. And driving around with Dr Keita that morning, I found it hard not to be moved by the ambition of the president, his wish to build and create to the highest standards he knew.

In his magnificence there was religion. Just as in some societies the peasant reserves his very best for his god, so here this striving after material splendour served the divinity that protected the kingship. Yamoussoukro was like the Pyramids or Angkor Wat. But these monuments, looking to the rulers' afterlife, had no purpose beyond themselves. Yamoussoukro was to be a living metropolis. It was to be the ruler's ennobling benefaction to his people, people of the West African forest, and – like the crocodile ritual – it was proof both of his right to rule and the justness of his rule.

Far down a wide, empty avenue we came upon a university or a centre of higher education. It had a freestanding, purely decorative arcade all around, as high as the building itself. The arcade was faced with brown mosaic. Great walkways linked the four quarters of the main building. There was an Olympic-standard swimming pool (showing, already, some signs of neglect). There were dormitories for students, houses for faculty staff. And just a little way down the avenue was another, complementary educational complex.

How many students attended the university? Someone said six hundred; somebody else said sixty.

The metropolis of Yamoussoukro awaited full use. But it had been created by foreigners. It was something that had been imported and paid for; and modern buildings like the university were not simply physical monuments that would last; they were like pieces of machinery, liable to decay. The new world existed in the minds of others. The skills could be learned, but faith in the new world was fragile. When the president went, and the foreigners went away (as some people wanted them to), would the faith survive? Or would Africans be claimed by another idea of reality?

In the slave plantations of the Caribbean Africans existed in two worlds. There was the world of the day; that was the white world. There was the world of the night; that was the African world, of spirits and magic and the true gods. And in that world ragged men, humiliated by day, were transformed – in their own eyes, and the eyes of their fellows – into kings, sorcerers, herbalists, men in touch with the true forces of the earth and possessed of complete power. A king of the night, a slave by day, might be required at night never to exert himself; he would be taken about by his fellows in a litter. (That particular fact, about a slave king, came out at an inquiry into a slave 'revolt' in Trinidad in 1805.) To the outsider, to the slave-owner, the African night world might appear a mimic world, a child's world, a carnival. But to the African – however much, in daylight, he appeared himself to mock it – it was the true world: it turned white men to phantoms and plantation life to an illusion.

Something of this twin reality existed at Yamoussoukro. The metropolis, the ruler's benefaction to his people, belonged to the world of the day, the world of doing and development. The crocodile ritual – speaking of a power issuing to the president from the earth itself – was part of the night, ceaselessly undoing the reality of the day. One idea worked against the other. So, in spite of the expense, the labour, the ambition, there was a contradiction in the modern pharaonic dream.

The crocodiles – I hadn't heard about them until I had got to the Ivory Coast. And now that I had seen them I kept on hearing about them. Everything I heard added to the religious mystery. I heard about one of the palace watchmen who had been killed on the sandy bank beside the causeway. A crocodile had laid its eggs in the sand. The watchman didn't know. He walked past the spot. The crocodile rushed at him and seized him and dragged him into the water. There was another story about a man, a villager, who had fallen over the iron rail into the lake and had been mangled by a crocodile, as the black chicken had been mangled. Was that an accident? Or had the man been pushed, a forced sacrifice? That was one view. The other was that the man was a voluntary sacrifice, that he had been persuaded (perhaps by some threat) to do what he had done in order to save his village from some evil.

So the crocodiles – seen in daylight, by a crowd with cameras – became more than a tourist sight. They became touched with the magic and power they were intended to have, though the setting was so staged: the broad avenue lined with lamp standards, the artificial lake (no doubt dug with modern excavators), the iron rails, the presidential guard with guns. The long-gowned feeder and the grey-suited official with him, when I called them back to mind, were especially unsettling. The official had smiled and clucked at the crocodiles, as though he knew them well, as though they were on his side.

And the symbolism remained elusive, worrying. Did the feeding ritual hold a remnant of ancient Egyptian earth-worship, coming down and across to black Africa through the Sudan? In a famous papyrus scroll from ancient Egypt, a woman in a plain white smock, hair undone, is shown bowed down before the crocodile, both on the horizontal line representing the earth, the horizontal line resting on the chevrons that in Egyptian art depict water. Or was the symbolism simpler? A crocodile was the strongest creature in water; it was universally feared; it lived long; it slept with its eyes open. And what was the significance of the hen? Was it an enemy? Or did it stand for reincarnation, as some people said: new life daily given to the crocodile, emblem of the ruler's power? Perhaps the concepts were not really translatable.

Outside the town, we came upon another kind of order, another kind of power: the president's agricultural estates. They went on for miles and miles: the disorder of dark tropical forest replaced by levelled, sun-struck fields, where mangoes, avocadoes and pineapples grew in rows. How had the president come by all this land? Had he converted unused, unclaimed forest into private land? Or did he as chief own all the land of his tribe? No one that morning seemed to understand my question; and the answer was no longer important. Two years before, the president had given his estates to the state. Like Yamoussoukro itself, it was a benefaction, a model for the future, and part of the ruler's religious sacrifice.

Doubly religious was the great mosque of Yamoussoukro. It was at once a gesture to the Muslims among the population, and the ruler's offering to another aspect of divinity. The mosque was square-towered, not fine in its detail, and I was told it was in the North African style, North Africa being the source of what was Islamic in this part of Africa. North Africa, France: the African ruler, aiming at material splendour, had to look outside black Africa. It was part of the pathos of Yamoussoukro. The mosque, off a wide, unfilled avenue, was in a big, bare yard, open to sun and the harmattan. Like many other buildings in Yamoussoukro, it appeared – perhaps wrongly – to await full use. It felt like a shell; it was possible, in the barrenness of its unwelcoming yard, to see it as a ruin. But it was big, and it was one of the sights.

We had a late lunch at the golf club. Ibrahim Keita and an Ivorian banker were our hosts. Ibrahim, after his day on the course, was fatigued and said little. The architecture was in the luxurious and playful international style. The menu was French, too ambitious for its own good; the waiters were uniformed. Yamoussoukro might have been only a playground, a tourist spot. But we who were there were living out the president's ambitions for his ancestral village. We were, whether we liked it or not, in his religious embrace. In another part of the metropolis, in an hour or so, the crocodiles were to be fed again.

There were many cars on the road back to Abidjan: people returning to the other world from villages that were as sacred to them as Yamoussoukro was to the president. It was the end of the public holiday, the twenty-second anniversary of independence, celebrated by white, green and saffron flags everywhere, and coloured portraits of the very small, benign man who had ruled for all that time.

11

In Abidjan I met a middle-aged European who had worked all his life in Africa and had lived for many years in the Ivory

Coast. He worked in the interior. His job was rough, un-intellectual. He had little social life; and unlike the other expatriates I had met, he spoke about Africa without any obliqueness. He said, 'All that you see here in Abidjan is make-believe. If the Europeans were to go away it would all vanish.'

Africans, he said, were still ruled by magic. In the interior, when a chief or an important local man died, the man's servants and his wives were buried with him. If the servants had run away at the time of the death, then heads were bought. That explained the regular disappearance of children, as reported in the necrology page of the newspaper. On that page there was a coded way of referring to certain kinds of death. A death by poisoning was said to have occurred 'after a short illness', *après une courte maladie*. A child reported as having disappeared was presumed to have been sacrificed. In the interior, for these funeral or other sacrifices, a head could currently be bought for 10,000 francs, less than £20. Not long before, in the area where this European worked, an important local man died. Heads were needed – the man was very important; and the panic was so general that for three weeks no worker turned up for the night shift at the factory the European managed. At certain ceremonies of welcome a chief or an important man had to have his feet washed in blood. Usually it was the blood of a chicken or an animal. But to do a chief the highest honour, his feet should be washed in human blood, the blood of a sacrificed person, a child. And the child could be eaten afterwards.

I believed what this man said. He liked living in Africa; he had worked nowhere else; he could work nowhere else. His directness came from his acceptance of African ways. He was not concerned to score points off Africa. But his acceptance went with a correct distancing of himself from the continent and its people. And for him that perhaps was the charm of the expatriate life: the heightened sense of the self that Africa gave.

It was of that kind of expatriate that I heard not long afterwards from a young American lawyer. He worked for an international law firm and was posted in the Ivory Coast. Business sometimes took him to Zaire, the former Belgian Congo. The Zaire boom of 1971 and 1972 was long past, the lawyer said; but there were now more expatriates than ever in the country – Indians, Greeks, Lebanese. They were people hooked on the way of life. They liked living on the edge of Africa, as it were, at the extremity of their own civilizations. They knew how to manage in the country; they liked that too, that idea of knowing how to manage. Some did well; some ended badly; most just carried on.

Recently the lawyer had been to Zaire to make an inventory of the effects of an elderly American who had died. The American had gone to the old Belgian Congo in the 1930s, and he had stayed there through everything, colonial rule, the second world war, Congolese independence, the civil wars. He had spent his last years in a one-bedroomed flat in Kinshasa. He was worth about a million dollars, but the personal possessions he had left behind were few: two suits, four pairs of trousers, a couple of pairs of shoes. He had done nothing big or adventurous. His business dealings had been simple, small, mainly in property. He had never used the money he had made. It lay idle in banks, in stocks. He had stayed in the Congo because he had been hooked on the life.

The young American lawyer didn't try to define the

glamour of the life. But I thought it would be something like this: being in Africa, being a non-African among Africans. Discomfort and danger would add to the sense of the self, the daily sense of personal drama, which a man living safely at home might never know. Africa called to people for different reasons. Everyone who went and stayed had his own Africa.

And then – after Yamoussoukro and the crocodiles, and what I had heard (and believed) about the heads – I had a bad night. I dreamed I was on a roof or bridge. The material, of glass or transparent plastic, had begun to perish: seemingly melted at the edges. I asked whether the bridge would be mended. The answer was no. What had been built had been built; the roof or bridge I was on would crumble away. Was it safe, though? Could I cross? The answer was yes. The bridge was safe; I could cross. And in the dream that was the most important thing, because I wasn't going to pass that way again.

The buildings of Abidjan, seen in the morning mist of the lagoon, seemed sinister: proof of a ruler's power, a creation of magic, for all the solidity of the concrete and the steel: dangerous and perishable like the bridge in my dream.

12

Andrée, Arlette's friend and fellow West Indian, telephoned from the university. Andrée's message was that her *patron*, Georges Niangoran-Bouah, the Drummologie expert, had returned from the United States. He sometimes went there, to universities that offered courses in 'black studies'.

When I went to the little office in the Institute of Ethno-sociology I found a big and very black man, filling the big swivel chair behind the big desk. Without him, when Andrée was there alone, with her knitting, the office had seemed widowed. He had the physique of a chief, heavy flesh on his chest, folds of fat on his stomach; and the light-grey, short-sleeved sports shirt did not hide his size. His French, though accented, was clear and precise. His manner, a lecturing manner, was that of the French academic. He had been publishing sociological papers for twenty years. The note I had had about him said he was fifty-five; but he looked ten years younger.

He was pressed for time – he should have been with a class. But he outlined the ideas behind his Drummologie studies. The earliest European travellers in West Africa didn't know African languages. So, though they observed a lot, they also missed a lot. They were wrong about the talking drums. The drums didn't invite people to special feasts or beat out messages through the bush: 'A white man is coming'. Drums were far more important than that in West Africa. To Africans it wasn't the word that existed in the beginning; it was the drum. Africans said, 'In the beginning was the drum.' Drumming, and the chanting that went with it, were special skills, handed down through the generations. The drum mimicked human speech; a trained singer could re-discover, in a particular passage of drumming, a poem, an incantation, a piece of tribal history, a story of victory or defeat.

Drums were sacred objects, symbols of the king, the tribe, the state. And Mr Niangoran-Bouah opened his book and showed photographs of famous tribal drums to prove his point. One drum was hung with jawbones, another hung with *cervelles*, the brains of enemies, wrapped up in skins. That was how important drums were to the tribe. Another photograph showed the great royal drum of the Baoulé people, the Kwakla drum, matted with the blood of many sacrifices. Some drums were so sacred they weren't allowed to rest in the ground. There was a recent photograph – taken by someone from the Institute of Ethno-sociology – of a drumming-and-singing ceremony in which the great drum rested on the head of a slave – or so Mr Niangoran-Bouah said.

The man said to be a slave was a muscular, shifty-looking fellow. He looked shifty perhaps because of the camera, at which he was glancing out of the corner of his eye; perhaps because of the weight of the drum and the din of the drum-beat just above his head (a small, bright-eyed old man, standing behind the drum-bearer, was pounding away with sticks on the drum); and perhaps because while the other men, elders and performers, wore their African cloths off the left shoulder, he, the drum-bearer, had to bare his chest and – in addition to supporting the drum with his left hand – had to keep up his cloth just above his waist with his right hand.

Mr Niangoran-Bouah found the photograph full of interest. He clearly relished these ceremonies, coming down from the African past. Pressed for time as he was, he examined the photograph in detail with me, and said, 'If the slave drops the drum he will be killed.'

I said, 'Killed?'

'But yes.' Then he qualified what he had said. 'In the old days. Today they would probably sacrifice an ox or an animal.'

'Are there still slaves in the villages?'

Mr Niangoran-Bouah said in his lecturer's manner,

'Slavery is of two sorts. In matrilinear societies slaves are taken into the tribe. They father children for the tribe. In patrilinear societies slaves are – slaves. Today of course there are no slaves. But' – and Mr Niangoran-Bouah smiled and threw back his chest and something of the chief's grand good humour came to him – 'a man in a village cannot conceal his ancestry. Everybody knows that this one or that one is the son or grandson of a slave.'

Somebody, a colleague or a student, came into the office and said that the class was waiting, had been waiting for half an hour. Mr Niangoran-Bouah stood up, gave me an appointment for a few days ahead – he wanted to play me a few recordings of drums – and went off to his lecture on some aspect of African civilization.

I had dinner at the Brasserie Abidjanaise. The French proprietress was soft and large and lacy, dreamy-eyed but commanding. She made me feel I had to be careful. The uniformed waiters, deferential to her and her ideas, were stern about the ritual of the house. The big balloon glasses were for wine, and wine was to be drunk only out of those glasses: I hadn't, after all, been careful enough. Later, at the Forum Golf Hotel, it was the Soirée Africaine: seven topless, big-breasted girls dancing to the sound of drums in La Cascade, the garden restaurant beside the swimming pool. Always, in Abidjan, these two holiday Africas, the French and the African. And the African was more real and rooted than might be supposed.

Andrée sat at her desk by the window and did her knitting. With Mr Niangoran-Bouah in his swivel chair, the scene was almost domestic. (The influence of literature, the influence of the French language! I saw Andrée as French; and fleetingly, though knowing it to be absurd in the setting, I saw her as a Balzac character.)

Mr Niangoran-Bouah was in the same grey sports shirt. He had a big tape-recorder on his desk; he was ready to play his recordings. But I had heard a fair amount about the drums, and I wanted him to talk instead about burial customs. I thought the subject might be a touchy one, but Mr Niangoran-Bouah was only too willing to talk about burial customs. He was fascinated by all aspects of traditional African life, and his attitude was purely descriptive. He didn't seem to think that these African things had to be either judged or defended.

When a big local planter died, his foreign labourers panicked and ran away. Mr Niangoran-Bouah told this as a funny story. '*Ils se sauvent*.' 'They scamper.' And he slipped one open palm off the other to suggest people running away fast.

African burial customs, he said, were like those of ancient Egypt. People believed that after death they continued the life they had lived on earth. So a man needed his wives and servants to go with him when he died. Some wives and servants understood this and accepted their fate. For those who didn't want to be buried with their master there were sanctuary villages. Mr Niangoran-Bouah drew a rough diagram on the back of an envelope. This showed that for every village there were, at different points of the compass, and within easy reach, four established sanctuary villages. But wives and servants looking for sanctuary had to be sharp. They had to get out of the way before their husband or master died. Once they had made it to a sanctuary village

and claimed the protection of the chief there they were safe.
Still, not everybody could be trusted these days, and there
could be accidents. That was why the government had decreed that the burial of chiefs and other important men should
take place publicly. That was why there was so much about
funerals on television and in the newspaper.

It was a poor life in the spirit world, Mr Niangoran-Bouah
said. He spoke with feeling; I was surprised. He forgot his
good humour, his lecturer's manner. The dead needed money
from the living. The dead had no clothes, had no money
to buy clothes, and they were cold – and Mr Niangoran-
Bouah plucked at his own grey shirt. The dead had no food
and were hungry – and the big man made a gesture with his
fingers of taking food to his mouth. Because life in the spirit
world was so wretched, Africans couldn't really believe in
the Christian after-life. For Africans the good life was here
and now, on earth. The end of that life was the end of
everything good.

'So African Christianity is an African religion?'

Mr Niangoran-Bouah said, 'I am a Christian. The first in
my family. But I am attached, profoundly attached, to
African animist belief.'

Djédjé, an altogether simpler person, had said much the
same thing.

Arlette came into the office. She was chewing an aromatic
gum, and she sat and talked quietly with Andrée, out of
whose silent, busy knitting needles, and subdued 'nervous-
ness', there was emerging a fantastically coloured little
garment.

With a quarter of my mind, while Mr Niangoran-Bouah
talked, I wondered – so far, after Yamoussoukro and the

crocodiles, and the heads, and my own dream about the decaying bridge and general dissolution, had I been drawn into Mr Niangoran-Bouah's spirit world – I wondered how Arlette had, as if in a novel or a play, and at another level of reality, walked into the office at that moment. And then I remembered. Arlette and Andrée were not only compatriots and friends; Arlette had also arranged my meetings both with Andrée and Mr Niangoran-Bouah; Arlette worked in the university.

But if the here and now was all that mattered to Africans, as Mr Niangoran-Bouah said, how did magic and the gods and the spirits fit in? Was it my own fantasy, that idea I had had of the two worlds in which Africans lived? Or was that double or twin reality something associated only with the lost slaves on the other side of the Atlantic?

I tried to find a suitable question.

I said, 'Is it real for Africans, the European world? This city they have built here in Abidjan – do Africans consider it real?'

And I was so taken by what Mr Niangoran-Bouah said that I asked for a sheet of paper to write down his words. Gently, like someone performing a welcome domestic duty, Andrée put down her knitting and gave me three sheets of thick new paper.

I wrote: 'The world of white men is real. *But, but*. We black Africans, we have all that they have' – and Mr Niangoran-Bouah meant aeroplanes, cars, rockets, lasers, satellites – 'we have all of that in the world of the night, the world of darkness.' '*Le monde des blancs est réel. Mais – mais – nous avons, nous autres africains noirs, nous avons tout cela dans le monde de la nuit, le monde des ténèbres.*'

So that at night Africans today – like the slaves across the Atlantic two hundred years ago – lived in a different world.

Arlette, still chewing – but gripped now by our conversation, since Andrée had broken off to give me the paper – Arlette, eyes bright, said, '*Ils pratiquent la nuit.*' 'They do it all at night.'

And in some ways Africans had exceeded Europeans, Mr Niangoran-Bouah said. Europeans could achieve only limited speeds, even with their rockets. Africans existed who could convert themselves into pure energy. Such an African might say, 'Let me be for a while.' And when after a second or so of concentration he came to again, he might give you news of Paris. Because in that time he had been to Paris and come back; and he had talked to people in Paris. So, without leaving Africa, a man might see his son in Paris and talk to him. But there could be no touching during those meetings. The man in Africa wouldn't be able to touch his son in Paris, because a man could maintain his physical footing in only one place.

'They have doubles,' Arlette said. 'They send their doubles. That is why they cannot touch.'

'There are people in the villages today,' Mr Niangoran-Bouah said, 'who can give you news every night of Paris and Russia. And they are certainly not getting it on the radio.'

Arlette, explaining this African gift, spoke of the Dogon people in the north. They had a great knowledge of astronomy, especially about the star Sirius, and they were said to be in touch with extra-terrestrial spirits.

So the world absolutely changed at night for Africans?

I understood Mr Niangoran-Bouah to say that it did. 'We say that a woman is stronger at night than a man.' '*La femme la nuit est plus redoutable que l'homme.'* 'The sick beggar you see begging alms all day on the pavement is really in the world of the night a great dignitary.' *'L'infirme ou le malade mendiant que nous voyons tout le jour sur le trottoir en train de demander de quoi vivre est en réalité par le monde de la nuit un grand dignitaire.'*

The electric light in the office went out.

Mr Niangoran-Bouah, jovial, made a French exclamation. *'Catastrophe!'*

Andrée was reminded by the power failure that she had to make a telephone call. But now, she said, because the electricity had gone it wasn't possible. Mr Niangoran-Bouah said the telephone worked on a different line. So Andrée put down her knitting and dialled. But the telephone, though working on a different line, gave trouble.

Mr Touré, the head of the Ethno-sociology Institute, not a big man, slightly military-looking in his near-khaki safari suit, came in with some banknotes in his hand. He gave the notes without ceremony to Mr Niangoran-Bouah and Mr Niangoran-Bouah – rather like the village chief at Kilometre 17 – held the notes in his hand while he talked.

I asked, 'When does the world of the night begin?'

Mr Niangoran-Bouah said slowly and seriously, 'As soon as the sun goes down.'

Arlette said that in some parts of Abidjan electric light was altering the hours of the night, and interfering with the powers that came into play. There was a friendly altercation between Arlette and Mr Niangoran-Bouah about this. I got the impression that Mr Niangoran-Bouah was saying that electricity made no difference to the night world.

He went on to tell a story about men who could make themselves all energy. The darkest time of the colonial period, he said, was during the second world war. And, as though the personal wound was still with him, he said it again, stressing the words: it was the darkest time. Arlette supported him. It was a time of forced labour; people were seized, as in the slave-catching days, and taken off to work on French plantations.

One old man was seized. He was bewildered; he didn't know what his captors wanted. They began to whip him. He said, 'Why are you whipping me?' They told him: 'We want you to carry this load to that place in the interior.' The old man said, 'Is that all you want? Is it for that alone that you are whipping me? To get this load to that spot? Well, if that is all you want, you go ahead.' They said, 'What do you mean?' He said, 'I mean what I say. You leave me here. You will get your load.' In the end they left the old man, thinking him mad, and when they got to where they were going –

'They found that he had got there before them,' Arlette said, finishing Mr Niangoran-Bouah's story for him, fixing me with her bright eyes, and nodding to the rhythm of her own words.

The old man had sent his double with the load. He had converted himself into pure energy.

It was a story that might have come from a Caribbean slave plantation two hundred years before. White men, creatures of the day, were phantoms, with absurd, illusory goals. Power, earth-magic, was African and enduring; triumph was African. But only Africans knew.

I asked Mr Niangoran-Bouah about the crocodiles of Yamoussoukro and the sacrifice of the live chicken.

I had seen him academic, good-humoured, tender, passionate, always open. For the first time now I saw him momentarily at a loss. The crocodile ritual was not something he was willing to talk about. He said, 'The crocodiles belong to the president.' He added, 'He feeds them.' Then he said, 'The emperor of Abyssinia also had certain animals that he fed.'

Arlette, eyes twinkling, said the emperor of Abyssinia always kept a little animal with him. That little animal was his fetish.

Mr Niangoran-Bouah didn't comment on that. He re-assumed his academic manner. He said, 'There are three symbols of kingship in Africa. On the savannah, the panther. In the forest, the elephant. In water, the crocodile. The crocodile is the strongest creature in the water. With one blow of that tail it can kill a man. Or' – and Mr Niangoran-Bouah brought his palm down sideways on his desk – 'it can break this desk.'

The crocodile was wicked, *méchant*. It especially hated the dog. It was suicide to try to cross a crocodile lake or river in a pirogue if you had a dog with you; the crocodiles would certainly attack the pirogue and overturn it. Crocodile-hunters used the carcase of a dog as bait. The crocodile couldn't live in salt water. There used to be crocodiles in the lagoon of Abidjan until a cutting was made to the sea and salt water was let in. Now there were no crocodiles in Abidjan, though recently there had been reports of sightings.

The crocodiles of the Ivory Coast: the more one heard about them, the more they held the imagination. And it became easier to accept, looking at Mr Niangoran-Bouah's photographs, that the swastika design on some Ashanti gold weights might have evolved from a simplified rendering of the crocodile: a creature all legs and snout and tail, murderous snout twisting or curving into murderous tail.

African art, African civilization, the density of African response: after his colonial wounding, that was Mr Niangoran-Bouah's cause. In the Ashanti weights there was the beginning of writing and mathematics. In the chants that went with the ritualized drumming there were the beginnings of history and philosophy.

On the desk there was the big tape-recorder. At last he played some of his precious recordings: first the tribal song or ballad, then the drums that mimicked the beat of the words. It was impressive. I began to understand the richness of the material he had made his subject, and his passion to present this material adequately to Africans and the world.

He was going off that weekend with thirty of his students to a village. The chief had invited them for the yam festival, *la fête des ignames*, an occasion so important that in some villages the sacred drums were brought out and played. In the village he was going to that weekend there were to be sacrifices of cattle, perhaps five or six. He was excited by the prospect of his weekend in the country. These old African rituals were as meat and drink to him. They were part of his past, his religion, his soul. He was also a writer and an academic, and these mysteries were among the many African things that awaited his pen and camera and tape-recorder.

But – thirty students in a village? Where were they going to stay? What arrangements would be made for them?

Mr Niangoran-Bouah said, 'Oh, there's a hotel.'

I said jokingly, 'So you are out in the field much of the time?'

He gave his chief's laugh. '*All* the time, *all* the time.' '*Toujours, toujours.*'

I left with Arlette. She admired Mr Niangoran-Bouah and

was pleased that the introduction she had brought about had worked so well.

I asked her about the crocodiles. 'What does it mean, Arlette?'

She said, 'Nobody knows. Only the president knows.'

From other people, Africans and Europeans, I heard more. I heard that before the president had dug his palace lake and put in his crocodiles, there had been no crocodiles at Yamoussoukro. I heard that the keeper of the president's crocodiles was the president's sister and that she was unmarried. I heard that crocodiles were more dangerous on land than in water; then I heard the opposite. I heard that the crocodiles of Yamoussoukro, by a particular movement of their heads, warned the president of danger to the state. And at the end I felt that it was as Arlette had said: the crocodiles, so feared, were meant to be mysterious, to be felt as a mystery, and only the president knew what they, and the ritual of their feeding, stood for.

13

On Saturday, while Mr Niangoran-Bouah was at his yam festival, Arlette went to Grand-Bassam, the old, abandoned (and in parts still derelict) colonial capital. In Grand-Bassam there was a vernissage – local painters, both white and black, and Haitian painters – in a restored, French-owned house of the colonial period. All cultural Abidjan was there – mainly expatriates, black and white; and in that cultural expatriate world Arlette was a figure. On Sunday Arlette went to Bassam again, in another party, for the expatriate Sunday treat of a swim in the ocean and a sea-food lunch in a beach restaurant.

She came back refreshed from that to take me in the evening to the house of Joachim Bony, *ancien ministre*, a former minister in the government, for an apéritif.

As a minister of education, Mr Bony had for some time been Arlette's *patron*, and she still held him in awe. She was unusually abashed in his presence, and very concerned for the dignity of the occasion. And it was only two days afterwards that I learned from her that, for allegedly plotting against the president, Mr Bony had been a political prisoner for five years, before being pardoned by the president.

Mr Bony lived in one of the richer residential areas of Abidjan: green streets, big houses, big plots. A gate, a drive, a modern concrete house, many vehicles. He came out to greet us, a gracious brown-skinned man in his late fifties. He walked with a limp; one foot was twisted. He took us up some steps that led directly from the garden to his sitting room. The furniture was modern, glass and steel, everything matching. He closed the aluminium-framed glass door and turned on the silent air-conditioning.

The other guests were an Ivorian doctor and his French wife, people in their fifties. Both Mr Bony and his Ivorian friend, the doctor, had gone to France in the same year, 1946. The friend had stayed in France for twenty-one years, in Toulouse. His wife was from Toulouse. He was black to Mr Bony's brown, and he was a physically bigger man. His wife said that when he had come back to the Ivory Coast from Toulouse he had spent more time in France than in Africa. But he had 're-integrated' himself into his family. He went to his ancestral village every weekend.

How did he spend the time there? He said he looked after his family land. On weekends, he said, he became a *planteur*. He added jokingly in English, 'Gentle-man far-mer.' Wasn't he a little detached now from African village ways and the religion that went with those ways? He said he wasn't a believer (he meant in African religion), but in moments of crisis – he spoke with some amusement – he found himself willing to turn again to old beliefs.

I asked Mr Bony about the president's crocodiles. (I didn't at that time know the story of Mr Bony's political fortunes.) He said – without awe, without hesitation – that the crocodile was the totemic animal of the president's family. His own family totem was the panther. He explained: the panther was prudent and – Mr Bony made a gesture with the fingers of his right hand – when he leapt he was sure.

Could a hen be a totem? Yes, the doctor said. Could a family change its totem? No, the doctor said. No, Mr Bony said; a totem was something inherited, something that came from way back.

Mr Bony's manner was like that: direct, gentle, matter-of-fact, unawed. And just as he was the first person I had met to give a straightforward explanation of the crocodiles, so he was the first to understand my question about the president's estates at Yamoussoukro. Some of the land would have been state land, Mr Bony said; some would have been family land. The president's family were much more than village chiefs. They were *sous-chefs* of a great African kingdom; they might be described as local viceroys. In the colonial time their power had been reduced. But they had retained their authority in the eyes of the people.

It was of religion that we spoke after the doctor and his

wife left. Religion was fundamental in Africa, Mr Bony said.
There were two worlds, the world of workaday reality and
the world of the spirit. These two worlds ceaselessly looked
for one another. '*Ces deux mondes se cherchent.*' Mr Bony didn't
speak of the world of the day and the world of the night. But
soon in his conversation the world of the spirit became the
world of the supernatural. The supernatural couldn't be
ignored, he said. He himself had had premonitory dreams of
the deaths of his parents.

Europeans were inventive, creative people. That had to be
allowed them. But because they stressed or developed only
one side of man's nature they seemed to Africans like children, and sometimes because of their talents they seemed like
enfants terribles. It had been especially dismal for him, when
he had travelled in the communist countries of eastern
Europe, to see men reduced to units, treated as economic
beings alone. That was why, though dependent on Europeans
for so many things, Africans thought of themselves as 'older'
than Europeans.

Apéritif time was technically over; and Mr Bony – as
gracious as Arlette would have liked him to be – sent us away
in one of his cars, through his watchman-guarded gates.

Two days later I heard about his political fortunes. It cast
an extra, retrospective dignity on the man. And this dignity
made more curious his interest in the supernatural.

The supernatural Mr Bony had talked about was not
specifically African. But in Africa you slid so fast, so easily,
into other realms. *Fraternité Matin*, continuing the government war against bad magic (and at the same time obliquely
spreading the word that in the Ivory Coast sorcery was a
thing of the past), was reporting on practices among the Bété

people. No one in Africa – according to *Fraternité Matin* – was thought to die naturally. A sorcerer was always thought to be responsible, and suspected people could be put to terrible trials to prove their innocence. They were made to wear the dead person's clothes; they were made to eat 'the mutton of death', mutton soaked in the juices of a putrefying corpse. Generally, among the Bété people, truth was obtained from suspected persons by dropping the sap of the 'gôpô' tree in their eyes: it was believed that the eyes of the innocent would not be damaged by the gôpô.

And there had come my way a story which I didn't know how to treat. A defective refrigerated container on the Abidjan docks – part of a cargo from the Ivory Coast to Nigeria – had begun to give off an offensive smell. The container had been opened; it was found to contain severed heads. Sacrificial heads, for export; technology at the service of old worship. Was the story true, or was it an expatriate-African joke? (The humour of both Africans and expatriates could have coincided in a story like this.) I couldn't find out. All I could find out was that stories of this nature – and all the stories about poisoning, burials, the disappearance of children – were possessed by most expatriates. They lived with this knowledge of African Africa. But the Africa they kept in their hearts, the Africa they presented to the visitor, was the Africa of their respective skills.

14

There were expatriates and expatriates. The latest group, of women, had come from Harlem in New York. Not all were

native-born Americans. Some, by their accents, had gone to
the United States from the smaller islands of the English-
speaking Caribbean. Another roundabout return to Africa:
and they had come to spread their own kind of Christian
worship. They had also come to Africa as to the motherland.
They were ill-favoured, many of them unusually fat, their
grossness like a form of self-abuse, some hideously bewigged,
some dumpling-legged in short, wide, flowered skirts. They
were like women brought together by a common physical
despair.

Perhaps at the back of their minds was the idea that, being
black, in Africa they could at last pass. But Africa was cruel:
the Harlem ladies were among people with a sharp eye for
tribe and status and physical carriage. Perhaps, with an
opposite impulse, they had seen themselves as Americans,
more advanced than the people left behind in the dark continent. But here too they were deceived: the Ivorians, when
not blasé, deep in their own world, had a curious racial
innocence. Whatever their motives, the Harlem ladies, having come to the Ivory Coast, had become shy. They seemed
never to leave the hotel. Sometimes they preached to waiters,
when they could catch a waiter alone; but generally they sat together in the lobby, and left their little tracts on the tables there.

The ladies were in the lobby – worn out from sitting, silent
from doing nothing, and yet of overwhelming presence –
when Arlette came for a farewell drink. We didn't stay in the
lobby. We went to the bar.

Arlette's Africa was so different from the Africa to which
the Harlem ladies had come. Shortly after we had met, she
had said, when she was speaking of the failure of marriages
between Ivorians and foreign women like herself, that to live

in Africa and to understand its ways was to have all your old ideas unsettled. And that, Arlette had added, was a good thing. It was of her African learning that she chose to speak on this last visit, at first in the bar, and later, in the lagoon dusk, on the bar terrace.

She spoke of the two worlds, the world of the day and the world of the night, the two ideas of reality that made Africans so apparently indifferent to their material circumstances. I had seen it in the Ivory Coast, she said. Men of wealth and position could return easily to their villages at the weekend, could easily resume the hut life, could welcome that life. She had asked people from Ghana, now in chaos: 'You were rich the other day. Now you are poor and your country is in a mess. Doesn't this worry you?' And they had said, 'Yesterday we were all right. Today we are poor. That's the way it is. Tomorrow we may be all right again. Or we may not. That's the way it is.' That was the way it was in the upper world. The inner world, the other world, continued whole. And that was what mattered.

I said, 'So it wouldn't matter to you if by some accident this city of Abidjan fell into ruins?'

Arlette said, 'No. It wouldn't matter. Men would continue to live in their own way.'

Some Frenchmen had come out from the bar on to the terrace, not warm now, the light a dusty ochre. They sat at the next table. They were businessmen. They took out papers and folders from briefcases and began discussions. One of the men became interested in Arlette. Exaggerating his attentions, he considered her legs, her big, full figure. She had her back to him and she didn't notice. She was talking, and eating nuts and crisps as she talked.

In one of the conference rooms of the hotel there was a business conference of some sort, with many white men sitting at tables, listening to a man lecturing before a board: phantoms, preparing plans for things that were one day bound to perish. The sun was sinking in the haze of dust: the harmattan, arrived at last on the coast. The lagoon was hazy; the far bank, lost in haze, was like a view from the temperate zone. To one side of the hotel works were going on in the grounds of new houses being built in this fast-rising area.

I said, 'Arlette, you make me feel that the world is unstable. You make me feel that everything we live by is built on sand.'

She said, 'But the world is sand. Life is sand.'

I felt she was saying what Hindus say as a doctrinal point, and feel as a truth in times of crisis: that life is illusion. But that was wrong: ideas have their cultural identity. And Arlette had arrived at her knowledge, her sense of the two worlds, by her interest in 'esoteric studies' and African magic. This knowledge had come from her admiration of African tribal life: the chief's gift of pardon, the annual ceremony of reconciliation, the initiation ceremonies in the sacred wood, when for three months seven-year-old boys were subjected to tests that gave them a new idea of the world and their place in it. The Hindu's idea of illusion comes from the contemplation of nothingness. Arlette's idea of sand came from her understanding and admiration of a beautifully organized society.

She spoke with passion; she spoke poetically. She nibbled all the time, and all the time the Frenchman at the other table was looking at her legs.

She had a high regard for the African wise man, the man venerated as the sage. There was such a sage at this moment

187

in Abidjan, in the African district of Treichville. He was very famous; the president himself would have liked to show him honour. But the sage preferred to live where he lived, in the courtyard of a simple house in Treichville. He said that if he moved to the middle-class area of Cocody the people who needed his help wouldn't be able to come to him. They would have to walk, not having money for taxis. And the watchdogs of Cocody would bite them.

Arlette said, 'Some time ago I went back to Martinique to see my parents. It was horrible for me. The people of the Antilles are sick people. Their life is a dream. I will tell you this story. The plane back – it was a special plane – was delayed for two days. And that made me distraught. My mother was hurt that I should be so anxious to get away from her. I love my parents, but my anxiety to get away from Martinique exceeded my love for my parents. They are small-minded people over there, broken down by their history. Life is so big. The world is so big, but over there if a man gets a little job in a government department he feels he has done enough with his life. They think they are superior to Africans. But their life is a dream.'

I asked her about Yamoussoukro. Why build that great city, if the world was sand?

She said, 'It is the president's attempt to integrate Africa into the modern world.'

And I thought she meant that to build a city like Yamoussoukro was not to accept what it stood for as the only reality. Ebony, the poet and civil servant, had hinted at something like that. Ebony's father had said to him, 'I am not sending you to the school to be a white man or a Frenchman. I am sending you to enter the new world, that's all.'

As we walked out we passed the Harlem ladies in the lobby.

Arlette said, 'We get so many people like them from the United States. Black people who come here to convert the Africans. They are like everybody else who comes to do that. They bring their own psychic sickness to Africa. They should instead come to be converted by Africa. They are mad.' *'Ils sont fous.'*

November 1982–July 1983